MINISTERING TO GOD: THE REACH OF THE HEART

MINISTERING TO GOD: THE REACH OF THE HEART

ISBN 1-886296-10-3
Printed in the United States of America

Third printing, December 1997

Arrow Publications
P.O. Box 10102
Cedar Rapids, IA 52410
Phone: (319) 373-3011
Fax: (319) 373-3012

This book is lovingly dedicated to my parents, Dick and Jody Larson:

- To Dad, whose godly character as a father has consistently revealed the fatherly character of God.

- To Mom, whose feisty Scottish soul responds to God with genuine fervor and childlike faith.

CONTENTS

FOREWORD

There is an eternal hope in this book which has its origin not from earth, but heaven. It is the Lord's own hope that the church, which He created to stand beside Him as His bride, will be awakened to her highest, most noble pursuit, that of Christ Himself.

I have known Vicki Brooks and her husband, Dr. Michael Brooks, since 1989. As the daughter and granddaughter of missionaries to Ecuador, Vicki is quite familiar with the responsibility of the church to find the lost, feed the poor, and befriend the hurting.

Yet, since I have known Vicki, without neglecting the needs of those around her, she has felt a deeper passion. It is from the well-spring of her love for God that she writes, guiding us back to the "first cause" of all good works. In these pages we transcend the immediate clamor of needy voices; we hear the voice of God.

Take time with each chapter. Don't just ingest facts and zoom into the rest of your day. The precepts contained within these covers are substantial; they are garments that the bride of Christ will wear in preparation for her Lord. Put them on.

If we will truly be the generation alive when Christ returns, we will discover that the high calling of the church is a life of ministry to Christ. We will know for ourselves the Father's pleasure as our hearts reach and touch the heart of Christ.

Francis Frangipane
author of *The Three Battlegrounds*
pastor at River of Life Ministries

ACKNOWLEDGEMENTS

This book is the product of many people's patience and prayer—particularly that of my husband, Mike. His wisdom, encouragement, and late-night talks (worked into an already overloaded schedule) have sustained me.

Our two sons, Nathan and Jordan, have bolstered me with their hugs and happiness, and little Zion, our soon-to-be-born baby, has been my constant companion throughout these past several months of writing.

Special thanks is also given:

♦ to Christy Dolan, who committed herself to prayer on behalf of this book even before the first chapter had taken shape. Her faithfulness has been a model for me as I write.

♦ to Francis and Denise Frangipane, whose years of friendship, encouragement, and pastoral leadership have formed the spiritual incubator within which these thoughts have matured and grown strong.

◆ to Lila Nelson, Meg Diehl, and Billie Barker for their skillful editing of the final manuscript. Thank you, Lila, for your painstaking attention to detail with the text—both in substance and layout; Meg, for your organizational insights, clarifying suggestions, and sensitivity to content; Billie, for your unique ability to hunt for and kill "clutter" words without altering meaning or style.

◆ to family and friends in Wheaton, Illinois; Saint Louis, Missouri; Philadelphia, Pennsylvania, and Cedar Rapids, Iowa, who read portions of the manuscript and offered many valuable suggestions.

Finally, and most importantly, I give grateful, loving praise to my God and King, Jesus Christ. Thank You, Lord, for filling first my heart, then my head, with the thoughts contained in this book.

INTRODUCTION

The word *ministry* means "to serve." Ministering to God, therefore, includes anything that is done as service to Him. Since our God is without need, we as Christians traditionally serve Him by serving someone else in His name. We minister to Him by ministering to the needs of those around us.

The purpose of this book, however, is to focus on that aspect of ministering to God that does not intersect with, nor depend upon, human need. I am specifically interested in that activity of the heart which is reserved for the Lord Himself.

This may seem like a strange time in human history to cut away and focus on ministering to God. With increased social and economic struggle on every continent—with tensions mounting, conflicts escalating, personal stress and physical violence spreading like cancerous growths throughout our cities—the cry of human need is stronger than ever before and our churches work ever harder to respond.

They work long hours managing food pantries, support groups, evangelism efforts, youth activities, Sunday services, visitation teams, mission fund-raisers, counseling programs, and social issue councils. Add to this the need to respond to random acts of violence and large-scale natural disasters, and we see that there is very little affecting our society that has not in some way become the concern of the church.

So why is now the time to talk about ministering to God? Surely our ministry to mankind keeps us busy enough. In fact, for many, the idea of finding time to pursue one more ministry is hard to imagine.

It is partly *because* we are so preoccupied ministering to the world around us that we must break free long enough to discover what it means to minister to God Himself. The Bible tells us to "not be weary in well doing" (Gal. 6:9 KJV)—but most of us are. Most of us are overwhelmed by the cries for help all around.

As veterans of too many daily demands and too many graphic newscasts, we're shell-shocked, tired, and looking for rest. We want to find a safe, quiet corner of the earth far from bomb blasts and dying children. We want a place of sanity and reasonable behavior—a place where love is stronger than hate, where kids go to school carrying books instead of weapons, where teenage boys attend football practice instead of Lamaze classes, and mothers give birth to drug-free babies.

Everyone, it seems, is looking for some kind of escape. Even the church—the army of God—is looking for relief. Just as overwhelmed as everyone else, it wanders among the wreckage of embattled lives while the global Goliath of human misery rampages at will. We don't know what to do in the face of such screaming, roaring need. It's too big and we're too small. This giant's terrifying, thunderous cry taunts us day after day, stealing our strength.

Only God can help us now. Only He is capable of cutting through this daily intimidation. So we call out to Him. We weep for our neighborhoods and intercede for our cities. We remind God of His promises and ask Him for relief. We awake to the power of prayer and embrace a common hope: God will respond; He will help us.

Our hope is not misplaced. God does hear and He does respond. The package His help comes in, however, is not all that we expect. God sends us, not a mighty, seasoned warrior, but a young, harp-playing shepherd; not a battle-proven champion, but a singer steeped in communion. Like Israel of old, in answer to our cry there's only a kid with a few smooth stones in his pocket—fresh from the fields of ministering to God.

History tells us this is not such an unusual move for God to make. He often uses unlikely candidates to challenge overwhelming enemies. He uses foolish things to confound the wise and calls for ministry to Himself even when it is most costly and least convenient.

God has done it before and, I believe, He's doing it again. Now, in *our* generation, in the face of everything we find most frightening and oppressive, God is once again looking for worshipers, not just warriors. Now, as in days of old, His eye searches for those who will, even with the clamor of war all around them, seek His heart—not just His rescuing hand.

Even with the mounting pressure for more church-based ministry to mankind, God wants churches that look to Him first and to everything else second. The Scriptures tell us He wants a royal priesthood, a holy nation, set apart for Himself (1 Peter 2:9). He wants a people of passion and purpose—those familiar enough with His ways to minister to His heart.

When God has this, it won't matter what the odds against us are. However unfit and unlikely we as His followers may be, if we take seriously our ministry to Him first, He will, in turn, equip us as we minister to others.

If we come to Him, God will not spurn our inexperience or youth. He will not turn us away. Instead, as with countless generations before us, ultimately *He* will be our help. His joy will be our strength; His strength, our joy. Pressing forward without fear, we will see His glory rise. Our arm will gain power, our aim will hold true, our small stone will fly, and our Goliath will fall.

V. Brooks
May 1, 1995

If the truth of God is disclosed and the glory of God is manifest in Jesus, then the truth of God must be this, and the glory of God must appear in this—that God so initiates and acts that He destines Himself to enter into passion, to wait and to receive.

—W. A. Vanstone

PART I

THE CALL

MY SONS, DO NOT BE NEGLIGENT NOW, FOR THE LORD HAS CHOSEN YOU TO STAND BEFORE HIM, TO MINISTER TO HIM, AND TO BE HIS MINISTERS.

—2 CHRONICLES 29:11

1

DISCOVERY

Any experienced gardener knows a variety of ways to prepare the earth and plant a seed. So does God. Often His spade is quick, smooth, and not too disruptive. On other rarer occasions, He arrives with shovel and hoe, ready to greatly trouble the tight soil of our soul. Like dagger thrusts His work is done, the earth turned and sifted, in preparation for a single, precious, deep-seated seed.

CHICAGO TRAFFIC was normal for 5:30 P.M. I sat staring at the bumper in front of me and listening to the muffled sounds of the freeway. I was staring and listening, but like every other trip to and from work that year, I saw and heard more of the traffic in my head than outside my car. Gripping the wheel with white knuckles had become my standard reaction to the turmoil within and without.

Regardless of how slowly the car was creeping along, my brain was always speeding. Total standstills on the Eisenhower Expressway were just a renewed opportunity for my mind to race forward, change lanes, dodge in and out, and cut off other slower-moving thoughts. This day was the same as every other. Over and over the same words collided within me, "There must be more. There has to be more . . . "

Actually, I was headed directly into what most 20-year-olds consider "more." I was engaged to be married. He was great, and we were sure we would be happy. He talked, I listened. I talked, he listened. It was a good relationship. So why was House of Brides the last place I wanted to pass on my way home at night? What was this fear that gripped me every time I thought about wedding cakes and diamonds, white lace and flowers?

Certainly, marriage to a fine Christian man would be meaningful enough to fill this widening gap in my gut. Surely the questions in my head would be answered, in time, if I just kept moving forward into life's inevitables. Since I didn't know then that it would be four more years before I met the man who was to become my husband, I tried to enter wholeheartedly into the season of this engagement. I tried to be carefree and in love, but like everything else that had touched my heart since my return from college, it brought pain instead.

Searing, gripping pain tore me apart inside. Accompanying the pain were all the hallmarks of an existential wrestling match. Overwhelmed by futility and loss, I felt the anguish of separation from

God. A fog of anxiety and fear settled over everything I did. Every decision was subject to indecision, every forward movement found me further and further removed from the things that had always given shape and meaning to my life.

Without warning, I was trapped in the book of Ecclesiastes. All was vanity. I would find myself absentmindedly repeating the words again and again, "There must be more. Surely we were born for something more." More than waking in order to work, working in order to eat, eating and sleeping in order to wake and work again. More than graduating to have a career, marrying to have children so they could eventually graduate, work, marry, and have children of their own. Suddenly the cycle of survival wasn't enough. Even the diverting, relatively sophisticated survival of the 1970s was not enough.

My pastor and a local counselor were in strong agreement with each other; suicide was no solution. I wasn't so sure. Somehow, in a strange, twisted way it seemed like the honest thing to do. I was already dying inside and it seemed like there should be some consistency in my actions. Why go on with plans for living and loving when life and love were not real to me anymore?

I felt completely cut off from God and all His purposes. My body moved by habit through the days and the duties of two jobs, family, friends, roommates, and church. My heart was in shock, my mind was at war.

Every time the car door closed and the engine started, I would begin the search all over again. Those forty-five minutes of solitude twice a day were my chance to look for clues. Relentlessly, my mind traveled back six months to June of 1974. What had happened? What set off this incredible heart-darkness? Why could I no longer sense God's presence or hear His voice? What had caused such a sudden decline in my otherwise "normal Christian life"?

Theoretically, if I could find the road into this mess, I could travel back out. But there was nothing. There were no breadcrumbs to follow and no memory of any one thing that had led me so far from home. Nothing situational or circumstantial could be reversed to make it all better; it had just happened. As if a switch had been flipped, I was suddenly asking questions I couldn't answer. They were classic: "What is the purpose of my life?" "Why do I exist?" "For what reason have I been created?"

Tradition has it that everyone who grew up parallel to Woodstock and Janis Joplin eventually asks these questions, but I'd hoped to escape. I was a Christian and it seemed that somewhere in the process of getting to know Jesus I should have already settled these issues.

This, then, was the crux of the crisis. I already knew Jesus as my Lord and Savior . . . what more could there be? In high school, I had been a "Jesus freak," not a flower child. I had been born on the mission field, raised in a Christian home, and surrounded by the things of the church since I was very young. Most important, I hadn't just inherited my faith in God. I had searched and struggled, scrapped and clawed my way to a living walk with Him. My parents didn't just talk about God's sovereignty; they believed in it and actively entrusted their children to His care. They knew that the four of us had to find our own way, so they set up a loving, faith-filled, Scripture-padded home and let us knock ourselves out.

Over supper, we would talk long and hard about the things of God. Then, there would be enough rest from human voices for us to hear Him speak. It was a perfect greenhouse for all the vegetation of my early growth. Seasons came and went in this place of nurture, until my roots showed beneath the pot and I was transplanted to something bigger—college.

At the end of my first year, I returned home to work for more money to go back. At least that was the plan before this drought hit. Instead, I was suddenly dry, dusty, and paralyzed by need. Overnight, all of my plans seemed senseless. I didn't need more political science; I needed to know why I was alive. I didn't want to sit in the dorm hallway in my pink bathrobe and fuzzy slippers eating popcorn and giggling past midnight. I didn't want to get married, either. I just wanted to hear God's voice again. But He was silent.

It was a strange way for Him to loosen deep, hardened soil, but it worked. I was desperate. I began to ask people, all sorts of people, why they thought they were alive. Exposing my struggle was difficult to do, but pride is a poor companion, and I was lonely, so I pressed on.

As I talked with one person after another over the following few weeks, one thing became increasingly clear—no one else seemed to have any answers, either. In fact, quite unintentionally, the question always shifted from "What is my purpose?" to "What are my goals?"

This was easier; we all had goals. For some, it was as simple as wanting to retire and see the grandchildren more often. For others, career and travel plans were the focus. The tenderhearted altruists just wanted everyone in the world to be happy. We all passionately desired that there be an end to hunger and war.

For fellow Christians, the answer seemed to be evangelism. They desperately wanted everyone to hear about Jesus. I agreed. This was no minor objective, but somehow it didn't seem to be the true end to the road of inquiry I had embarked on. I still sensed there was "more."

Having long since lost my ability to see the road, I groped along, blind to any real progress I might have been making. Thick fog continued to blanket everything around me and I fought to find my way back from a dark and distant exile. I was so disoriented and confused during those days that now, years later, only one clear recollection remains with me. I remember that, in my discussions as I pursued the ultimates of each person's stated goals, a light began to glimmer.

"Suppose you are retired and can see the grandkids every day," I would ask, "Now, why do you exist?" Or, "Suppose you've traveled and seen the world and have a wonderful career; in fact, let's just imagine that all war has ceased, famine has ended, and everyone is completely healthy and happy. All human need has been met. Now, why are you alive?" To the Christians I would say, "Suppose that somehow the household of faith is complete. Everyone who wants to know Jesus now does. Let's pretend there is no one left to evangelize. Now, why do you exist?"

For those not struggling with crisis like I was, these discussions probably led to more confusion than clarity. But for me, the slender shaft of light grew broader. Just by the silence that met these questions, my hunch was confirmed. Of course we had nothing to say! Of course we were silent as we grappled with eternity—we remained in the grip of all things temporal. What was there to say? Could those things we were most sure of, those measurable, quantifiable things that defined our days, ever really be enough to answer the heart's call for more? Could earthly activity, however noble and engrossing, be the only reason for which we had been summoned to this great green foyer called "life"?

Of course, there was more! There had to be. We who were created in God's image, eternal by nature, could surely expect some task to engage our passion and energy that was also eternal. We had to have been marked with a higher mandate than personal problem solving and global peacekeeping. Certainly we were born for more than fruitful function here on earth, more even than fruitful evangelism. We had been brought into existence for something much greater than I yet understood, but I sensed its nearness, and it was enough to keep me going.

ONE BRIGHT morning in the fall of 1975, it was over. As suddenly as I had gotten lost fifteen months before, I found my way back. I cannot account for the abruptness with which my struggle ended, but suddenly everything in me rested and became quiet. Like a badly tangled cord which, with one last, strategic jerk finally comes straight again, I found my way. I had my answer. It came, surprisingly, in the familiar formality of the Westminster Catechism of Faith:

> What is the chief end of man?
> To glorify God and enjoy Him forever!

Without warning, these steady words took on fire and life beyond anything syllables and script could contain. No longer was this simply some time-worn Presbyterian motto. Never again would these words be just passive print on a yellowing page. They became my lifeline and my link with everything that had meaning and substance. I saw, as if for the first time, words that I had read so many times before: "Thou art worthy, O Lord, to receive glory and honour and power: for thou hast created all things, and for thy pleasure they are and were created" (Rev. 4:11 KJV).

Searing a path straight to the core of my being, these words opened wide the deserted, darkened portions of my heart. Light flooded in, warmth returned, and I responded without restraint to the ancient call:

> "Bring My sons from afar,
> And My daughters from the ends of the earth,
> Everyone who is called by My name,
> And whom I have created for My glory,

Whom I have formed, even whom I have made.
The people whom I have formed for Myself,
Will declare My praise."

—Isaiah 43:6–7, 21

As if by reflex, my knees bent and my entire being bowed. What privilege, what high purpose, had been entrusted to fragile flesh! He who has His pick of solar symphonies had chosen mankind to sound His praises! This One whose glory is so flawlessly echoed by all the angelic host had turned His ear to hear our whispered worship! It is true, "The heavens declare the glory of God; and the firmament sheweth his handiwork" (Ps. 19:1 KJV), but His *image* rests on the sons and daughters of Adam.

This then, is our task. It is our unique privilege to provide heaven with an everlasting reflection of God's glory, a timeless tale of His amazing goodness to a weary, wrinkled race. From bodies that have been cursed with death, we speak of Life. With eyesight dimming to the light of our own sun, we can still see Him who is the Light of all the ages yet to come—a Light that casts no shadow.

With the same voices that call the earth to prayer, we call for heaven's attention and declare the witness of a waiting church. A people born of woman's womb, we have been reborn of the Spirit and the Word. We carry in our weakness the signature of Him who sustains all starry space, all hidden spheres.

This is our reason for living. We are "living stones" in an eternal temple, priests to a living God. To this priesthood we bring our greatest passion, our eager energy. Here, on this side of the grave, in full view of Satan and his forces and of God and His angels, we are clothed in our eternal mandate. It is here and now, while the darkness grows stronger and faith is still necessary, that the church must embrace her fundamental function: *She was brought into being to engage God's heart, not just to meet man's need.*

For centuries, the church has gloriously and sacrificially spoken to mankind about God. Now, as the end of the age draws near, we must pursue the heart of God with equal fervor and sacrifice. Yes, we must appeal to Him on behalf of humanity, but we must also seek Him for His own sake. This is what He longs for (John 4:23; 2 Chron. 16:9). This is the fellowship for which He gave His Son to the earth.

Once embraced, this fellowship with God will produce an earthly witness that no amount of evil can undermine. Out of this passionate exchange will emerge a people who are able to minister effectively to the needs of their neighborhoods because they have first touched the heart of their God. They will face without fear the turmoil of the lives around them because, with arrows drawn directly from *God's* quiver, they will pierce the hearts of men and women with *His* love. Yes, the church will continue to have a witness worthy of the name of Jesus—one that reflects His ministry to His Father—as well as His ministry to hurting humanity.

In the weeks that followed my freedom, I came to understand in a renewed and more powerful way that mankind is the special object of God's love and desire. We exist expressly for Him. We have been shaped by His hand for unique interaction with His heart.

Our purpose in life is not simply to leave a legacy of good works and kind living. Whatever worthwhile tasks and goals we may pursue here on earth, it is ultimately God's pleasure, not our productivity, that validates our existence.

Neither are we here just to secure our salvation far away from the heat of hell. We have been called to something higher than insuring an eternity spent in peace instead of pain. As those who have been created for God, the major thrust of our existence is not our safety, but God's glory.

God is the beginning and the end of this sovereign story. "And every created thing which is in heaven and on the earth and under the earth and on the sea, and all things in them, I heard saying, 'To Him who sits on the throne, and to the Lamb, Be blessing and honor and glory and dominion forever and ever' " (Rev. 5:13). *He* is our purpose, and He is enough.

AFTER MONTHS of turbulent preparation, the ground had finally been declared ready. I felt the finger of God push this single seed deep into my heart. It took root there in the fall of my twenty-first year and now, years later, I sit in the shade of a maturing truth.

"What is the chief end of man? To glorify God and enjoy Him forever!" With great rejoicing these words have become the theme of my existence. The woven word of God has wrapped me fully round and now I wear these simple sentences everywhere.

I never take them off. I sleep in the comfort of their closeness and walk with them through each new day. I never tire of their pattern. I attend christenings and funerals alike in this single garment; and in this I will be buried, for it is what I want to be wearing when I meet Him face-to-face. I am sealed for all of time in this apparel of praise, cloaked in the sure knowledge that I do not exist for me at all. I have been created for God.

2

YOU HAVE TO LOVE THE MUSIC

Whatever our individual ministries among men may involve, whatever earthly tasks God has given us to do, we carry in our hearts a collective, sacred song—one common to all Christians, sung purely for the pleasure of God.

AS I RUSHED down the shiny corridors of the University's music complex, quick blips of sound hit me from every doorway. Like turning the selection dial of a radio, I heard brief, broken-off snatches of music as I ran past dozens of practice rooms. Coming at last to a small auditorium, I searched for Eric.

Several years had passed since we last saw each other, but my tall, lanky cousin was unchanged. With an easy grip on his beloved trombone, he gave me a bony hug and a boyish grin. He looked all grown up in his suit and tie—all grown up, but still too young to be the guest musician at this master class.

Over the next forty-five minutes, however, as he and his accompanist moved through one increasingly difficult piece after another, I realized afresh what a masterful musician he is. Eric, a trombonist with the Philadelphia Orchestra, was on a brief tour of the Midwestern states and had stopped in Iowa City for this single, two-hour symposium.

As the last notes of a duet from Bach's Cantata #78 died away, Eric turned to the expectant young faces before him. Intense, bright-eyed trombone majors sat scattered throughout the room, eager for advice on joining the world of professional concert musicians.

Loosening the mouthpiece of his trombone, Eric slowly wiped it with a cloth.

"How many of you plan to pursue a career with a symphony orchestra?" he asked.

Everywhere in the room hands went up.

"OK," he said, glancing around, "of those who raised your hands, how many of you want to play in an orchestra because it seems like a decent way to make a living?"

Expressions turned quizzical and this time only a few students responded.

"How many want to play the trombone professionally because you're good at it?" Eric asked. "It's what you do best and you know that given the right opportunity you would succeed?"

Between quick sideways glances around the room, several more students made hesitant responses.

"All right, then," he nodded, "how many of you want to spend your life playing this instrument because you *love* it—you love the trombone and you can't imagine doing anything else. To you this is not just an instrument, it's a way of life. It's as dear to you as a part of your own body and, more than anything else, you want to spend the rest of your life playing it!"

Immediately the mood in the room shifted; enthusiasm surged. No one was hesitant now. Of course! This was the test of a true musician—love of one's instrument! This surely was the ultimate measure of motives. Everywhere, arms shot into the air.

Eric paused.

"That's good," he said, looking slowly from face to face, ". . . but it's not enough."

Startled, the students grew still. Like the gradual descent of a hundred helium balloons, limp arms sank slowly, silently, onto the seats.

"It's not enough to love your instrument," Eric repeated. "Loving the trombone is not enough to sustain you through the decades of stress and monotony of a symphonic career. If that's all you have, you won't make it—you'll burn out."

Turning to put his trombone in its case, Eric continued quietly but clearly, "To stay emotionally alive in a professional symphony orchestra, you have to love what the composer has written. You have to love the *music*!"

SO IT IS with the church. To stay spiritually and emotionally alive in the church that Jesus leads, we have to love the music He has written. Our part, our instrument, is vitally important, but it is only by loving the music that our hearts will stay engaged in the part we've been given to play.

The music of the church is a love song. It is a song of fiery devotion between a Father and a Son. From its melodic core comes the familiar, recurring theme of God's love for man. Like harmony written to complement an ever-present melody, God's love for humanity moves in and around the central theme of His love for His Son. The passionate affection that exists between God the Father and God the Son serves as the wellspring for all of God's compassionate interaction with mankind.

This, then, is the music of the church, not just that God so loved the world (John 3:16) that He sent His Son to die (John 12:24), but that the Son so loved His Father that He was *willing* to die (Luke 22:42; John 12:27–28). Jesus' highest aim was to satisfy not just mankind's need but His Father's heart.

Everything Jesus did on earth was sovereignly synchronized with the music of His Father's will (John 5:19, 30; 14:31). Every move He made was dependent upon the leading of the Holy Spirit. Father, Son, and Holy Spirit, the ancient Chord of Three, has never ceased to sound. Like God Himself, The Music has no beginning and no end.

This love song that the church has been commissioned to play was written long before she was ever born. It predates her and her salvation message. Long before the earth was created, long before mankind was made, The Music of the Godhead ran throughout the great unformed expanse that is now our universe (John 17:5).

Before anything was that now is, the molten melody of this ageless song erupted with volcanic force onto every uncharted pathway of space and surged, lavalike, through every cosmic corridor. Thick and pure, unrelenting and all-consuming, its river continues to run, hot with the fire of life, straight from the throne of God.

It is this music that Jesus played during His days on earth and it is this same music that we His followers now carry. As members of the body of Jesus Christ, we have been captured by the activity of His heart—ministering to His Father this living song. As joint heirs with Jesus we inherit the same relationship He has with His Father and, therefore, the eternal song He has always sung.

Yes, we as mankind are the much-loved beneficiaries of Jesus' provision and grace, but *God* is the unquestioned focus of Jesus' zeal (John 2:17). As important and prized as we are in the overall scheme of things, it is still for the pleasure of the Father that The Music is performed. Jesus still conducts His orchestra for the approval of an audience of One.

This book is about learning to love The Music. It is about learning to stay positioned before the Father the same way Jesus did—responding to Him first and to everything else second. It is about learning to reach past the pull of our own ministry among men, past the love that we may have for our own instrument, and embracing the heart of God.

Ultimately this book is about the church learning that the music she's playing is primarily for One audience and that, if played with passion and purity, it has the power to draw all men to the knowledge of Him.

3

Here and Now

As followers of Jesus Christ, our purpose and strength come from our communion with God, not from the Great Commission. God alone is our source, and He must be our focus. Nothing less than full, passionate fellowship with Him will ever empower what we do for Him (John 15:5).

SOMETHING about the *occasion* of our salvation is important to us. As Christians, we often find special comfort in being able to remember the time and place of our conversion—the specific moment when we passed from death to life. That moment becomes more to us than a tombstone marking our past—it becomes a touchstone, marking the promise of heaven that is yet to come.

So important is the memory of this moment to some that, if for any reason the exact time and date are in question, the "steps" of salvation are repeated. The required words are spoken and the formula is followed again—just to be sure. Sure of what? Sure of heaven. Sure of "being with Jesus someday."

Though the touchstones of our faith are important and used by God in our lives, it seems strange that we look to dates, times, and places to secure a reality that should be living like fire within us. Like a person checking his birth certificate to confirm the beating of his own heart, it's strange that we need to review over and again our initial steps into the kingdom of God as assurance of our presence there.

Other indicators of life should be evident—something of the very heartbeat of Jesus should echo within us. Something of the inhaling and exhaling of His Spirit with ours should speak to us constantly of our life in Him.

As essential as the moment of our salvation is, the ongoing reality of walking with Jesus should speak to us daily. There is no reason for us to have greater hope of knowing Christ's presence "someday" in heaven than we do of living in His presence here and now (Matt. 28:20; John 16:7–15). After all, this is where we met Him. Earth is where He first made Himself real to us. It is here that He told us He would never leave us nor forsake us (Heb. 13:5 KJV). Surely it is here, as well as in heaven, that He intends for us to know the reality of His presence.

I GREW UP reading fairy tales. When I was quite young I was given several large, beautifully illustrated volumes of tales from Russia, China,

England, Scandinavia, and India. I spent hours with these books piled high around me, reading and re-reading stories of great adventure and romance. Though exciting and varied in plot, the endings were always the same. Somebody good always got the girl and they rode off into the mist, never to be seen again. The story ended and they disappeared. All I knew was that they lived happily ever after.

It is tempting to live this way with Christ. It is tempting, at the point of our salvation, to ride off into an emotional mist and disappear. All is well with us. We found Jesus and have secured eternal life. We're "safe" and headed for heaven, so what more is there?

In the interim, we're not entirely sure what is expected of us. We know that the Bible speaks of spiritual priesthood, but we don't know what that means in relation to us. We know that we have been called to "abide in Christ," but we're not sure how that's done.

In many ways these things seem mysterious and out of reach. We long for a living intimacy with God and deeply desire a sense of His presence, but are baffled by the resistance we face as we try to find it. How can we approach Him with any confidence of securing the fellowship He offers? We've tried, but with little sense of genuine contact.

Most of us want a deeper interaction with God; we truly desire a more vital, spontaneous exchange of hearts, but have grown accustomed to silence instead. Our prayer times are lonely, our "quiet times," too quiet, and our Bible study, just that—study.

Though we know we will live in God's presence in heaven, we don't know how to live in His presence here on earth. Though convinced that we will sustain great intimacy with Him throughout eternity, we don't know how to attain such closeness here and now.

So, we wait it out. We fix our hope on the next life and expect that a magical, effortless intimacy with God will develop the moment we leave this world behind. Emotionally, we withdraw from the daily disciplines of relating to Jesus Christ and turn our attention instead to the demands of human need. We do this, not because it is our first and truest calling, but because the needs are obvious, tangible, and urgent. We can *do* something in response. We turn our heart toward relationships in which the interactions are "real" and forthcoming, and the results are quantifiable.

The only problem with this approach is that it does not satisfy the deepest desire of God's heart. It does not secure His full pleasure, because it does not account for the full mandate that is on our lives. We were created for fellowship and ministry to God (Isa. 56:6–7), not just to the world around us.

Because this is true—because we were brought into being to respond to His heart—God does not allow us to stay safely nestled in a pocket of earthly productivity untouched by intimacy with Him. He pursues us.

My husband and I know a pastor in Illinois who has a large, thriving church. Every week over 2,500 people attend the worship services. He leads a staff of ten associate pastors, presides over care groups, counseling services, and a Christian grade school. His pastorate is clearly marked with the traditional signs of accomplishment and success. There is, however, a deeper, more important ministry that undergirds the obvious, "successful" ministry that most people see.

Ever since he was a child growing up on a farm in central Illinois, this man wanted to be in the ministry—to serve God by serving people. So real was his dream that, as a teenager driving the family tractor, he spent hours preaching to the open fields.

Finally, after completing his education, he and a friend began a small, fledgling congregation. As co-pastor of this new little church, his dream began to take shape. Soon larger and larger crowds were gathering each Sunday morning. The fulfillment of his lifelong ambition seemed on the verge of realization, when suddenly everything came to a crashing halt.

Through a series of circumstances, God asked this man to give up his pastorate. During times of prayer, he clearly heard the Lord ask him to relinquish all of his work. The exact words God spoke to his heart were, "Would you be willing for Me to put to death your ministry?"

Days and nights of agonized struggle followed. "Lord!" he cried incredulously, "All I've ever wanted to do is be a minister to your people. Everything I've trained for is just beginning to happen. People are getting saved, the church is thriving, I'm preaching well, and hurting people are being helped. I'm doing all this for You! How can You want me to step down now?"

As unbelievable as it seemed, the crushing conviction of God's will grew inside of him until he faced the inevitable question: "Is it the ministry that I love or is it God that I love?"

Until now the two had seemed inseparable. To love God had always meant to serve people. It had always been a foregone conclusion that one begat the other. Now, everything was a tangle of mixed motives and fading dreams. Like an unbroken colt, his heart bucked and reared as it realized the size and weight of the load it was being asked to bear. Heaviness and grief settled on him. All of the fondly held promises for his future were being recalled.

God was demanding the life of this man's Isaac and, like Abraham before him, he responded with an act of worship. He relinquished his pastorate.

"Lord," he said, "I don't understand this; I don't know why You're requiring it of me, but I love You more than I love my ministry, so here it is. I give it back to you. If all I am ever allowed to do in Your kingdom is worship You, it will be enough. If no one ever hears me preach but You, it will be enough. My ministry to You is more important than my ministry to people."

That day, a true "minister of the gospel" was born—someone who ministers to God first and to people second. A year later, God restored this man to the pastorate and now he can look back over twenty-five years of God's continual provision and blessing.

With or without the blessings, however, this man knows he has been marked for life. He will never again be just a successful pastor; he will always be a full-fledged minister. Any weekday morning, before facing the needs of his people, he can be found on his knees in the church prayer room ministering to the heart of his God.

IT IS TRUE that the task of working to meet human need has been given to the church. The Scriptures are quite clear that we have been commissioned to touch the wounds of the world around us, but that is not all we have been empowered to do. We have been given authority to touch the heart of God. By virtue of our love for God we have been called to stand before Him as those who minister directly to Him (2 Chron. 29:11).

This is the same authority King David exercised as he ministered to God in the tabernacle. Though not a Levite and therefore not a priest, David pursued the presence of God with such tenacity that he was welcomed by God as a friend. For David, ministering to God was not a ritualistic, religious duty; it was an all-consuming way of life.

Long before he played his harp to soothe King Saul, David used it to minister to God in worship. Long before he was allowed to minister to his people as their king, David ministered to God as a hunted exile. Through countless psalms, David the shepherd sang of *his* Shepherd (Psalm 23), and David the warrior-king sang of his own invincible Warrior-King (Ps. 18; 62:1).

We get a clear understanding from Scripture that David's foremost passion was toward the God that he loved and served (Ps. 25:15; 63:11). Sheep or no sheep, kingdom or no kingdom, David's heart was ever fixed upon his God. Though he was not a priest, by virtue of his worshiping heart David carried a priestly mandate and eventually led all of Israel in ministry to God (2 Sam. 6). So real was his example of active, passionate pursuit of God that he is known simply by that title, David, "a man after His [God's] own heart" (1 Sam. 13:14).

Ministering to God was not just David's purpose in life; it was also his protection. By staying close to God in worship, David remained safe from the fear of mankind (Ps. 27:1–3). By ministering to God, he became acquainted with God's ways and loyal to His purposes.

This we see evidenced in his battle with Goliath. While fear of man paralyzed the whole of Israel's army, fear of the living God energized David and propelled him to victory in one of the most remarkable battles the world has ever seen (1 Sam. 17:20–51).

King Saul, by contrast, is not presented in Scripture as someone who ministered to God. Instead, he is seen as a man so preoccupied with himself that he stayed safely clear of any extravagant, personal interaction with God. His own inadequacy, not God's sufficiency, became the primary focus of his attention.

Though anointed with the Holy Spirit, favored by God with kingship, and entrusted with the welfare of Israel, Saul's anxious, vain heart finally folded in on itself and he became a tormented, demonized man. Insecure, self-absorbed and afraid, Saul eventually succumbed to the will of the people he ruled instead of to the God that he served (1 Sam. 13:8–14).

By the end of his reign he had no ministerial role in Israel—not to his people, not to his God. In fact, by the end, Saul knew God in only remote, secondhand ways, and it wasn't enough to save his kingdom or his life.

From the lives of these two kings we can draw this conclusion: Regardless of how well positioned or equipped someone may be to minister to mankind, if they wish to do so in the *name* of God, they must first know the *heart* of God. And, if they are to truly know the heart of God, they must put their ministry to Him before all other things.

This is true for every believer, not just for the kings of ancient Israel. All Christians are, by definition, ministers to God first—then to mankind. The Scriptures tell us that the first and greatest commandment is to "love the Lord your God with all your heart, and with all your soul, and with all your mind, and with all your strength" (Mark 12:30). The second is to "love your neighbor as yourself" (Mark 12:31).

Our ministry to God is eternal in nature and requires the ongoing gift of our heart for the sole purpose of His pleasure. Our ministry to mankind, though important in its own right, must always be the result of our communion with God, never the other way around.

Any work that we do among men, women, and children here on earth must emerge directly from our intimacy with God. Nothing less can sustain it (John 15:4–7). Any comfort we give, any help we offer, must always be colored by our contact with God's heart. Everything we do to fulfill the second commandment must always pass through the filter of the first.

IT FOLLOWS then that, though we may find it more convenient to skip the demands of a current, daily interaction with God, He does not. While our own expectations of intimacy may be allowed to slumber until "someday," His never will. His intentions toward us remain compellingly present tense.

God's heart is not passive as He calls forth His priesthood—those who minister to Him. The fire of His own expectation is not tempered by the passage of time, for He knows there is no reason to wait. All has been accomplished. Everything that is necessary was acquired for us at Calvary. The price was paid, access to His presence was purchased (Heb. 10:15–22), and the door stands open for His priesthood to enter.

So it is that God insists on something unique, current, and personal from each of us. He requires that *who we are* interact with *who He is*. He asks for something from us that we can't hang a date on and tuck away in our spiritual hope chest. He wants more than a moment in time when we agreed to His conditions, shook hands, and promised to meet again in heaven.

If it is, therefore, our intention to fill heaven with endless concerts of praise, we start here on earth. If it is we who desire to share the dwelling place of the Most High God, we begin now! If eternity is ours, so is the present!

Now is the time to approach God with courage; now is the time to enter His nearness—here, in this life, without waiting for death to "free" us. For if Jesus is our Savior and Lord, then we have already died with Him and are already free. We are, in fact, by God's own proclamation, a "royal priesthood, a holy nation" (1 Peter 2:9), equipped and set apart for Him alone. We minister to the heart of God here and now, not just in the age to come!

IN THE NEXT CHAPTER we will see that it is God Himself who makes our ministry to Him possible. It is He who gives us strength to carry out all that He has commissioned.

4

MINISTERING TO GOD

Ministering to God is different from ministering to mankind. Traditionally, when the church ministers to people, it targets a point of need and tries to meet it. If someone is hungry they are fed; if sick, they are prayed for; if lonely, visited. Wherever the need is, there the ministry takes place.

Our God, however, has no needs. Though He desires our fellowship, He is complete without it. Though His heart is passionately involved with His people, He is not dependent upon them. How then do we "minister" to Him?

THE BATTLE had been raging for months. During that time the fighting had grown so fierce, so deeply divisive, that even family members stood opposite each other on the battlefield.

"Why are you here?" snarled Ares to his sister. "You tried to wound me once before—well, now it is my turn!" Raising his sword, he struck a crushing blow to Athene's head. Her helmet, however, was of special metal and the blow was repelled.

Seething with hatred, Athene struck back. Flinging a huge boulder, she hit her brother in the neck. He staggered under its impact and fell. "You silly fool!" she spat derisively. "You want to fight with me and you don't even know that I am stronger than you!"

Just then the beautiful Aphrodite ran to Ares' side. Taking him by the hand, she led him from the battlefield. Further enraged by this act of intervention, Athene ran after Aphrodite and knocked her down.

"Ha!" she exclaimed as she stood over her battered rivals, "If we immortals had fought, the war would have been over long ago, and Troy would no longer be standing!"[1]

THE ABOVE interaction is not a violent domestic dispute between human beings, but the bloody bickering of three Greek gods warring over the city of Troy. Far from the noble, majestic bearing expected of supreme beings, this kind of behavior

---

[1] Adapted from Homer's *The Iliad and the Odyssey* (New York: Dorset Press, 1991), p. 68.

was common among the deities that the Greeks and Romans worshiped.

The gods of these ancient empires were famous for their petty rivalries and moral indiscretions. Mythology is filled with accounts of their jealous rages, adulterous liaisons, schemes to injure and discredit each other, and elaborate plots of revenge for slights suffered. All in all these gods, though empowered with various supernatural attributes, were more human than godlike in character and temperament.

In like manner, ancient Babylonian gods had basic, physical needs that mirrored the human frailty of those who served them. Every day, priests would bathe, clothe, and feed the idols they worshiped. The Babylonians believed that the essence of any god they served lived inside their carved image of it. An idol was not just an earthly representation of a higher, heavenly being, but the actual body of a god.

Because of this, great care was given to the image itself, and no detail was overlooked in providing for its comfort and upkeep. Several times each day trays of food and flowers were brought to its chamber, holy water was sprinkled to purify its surroundings, and curtains were drawn to protect its privacy while eating.

Other cultures of the time worried about the health and strength of their gods. For instance, many sun-worshiping, agricultural societies would watch with great concern the apparent waning of their god's energies during the winter solstice. Pale and weak after the blazing work of summer, the winter sun gave an anemic, shallow warmth. Ultimately it seemed clear to the concerned worshipers that their god was either sick or dying.

Anxious to restore the sun's failing energy in time for the upcoming season of fertility and growth, a strong, virile young man or fertile young woman was ceremonially killed and their blood was offered to the sun god to drink. In this way it was thought that the sun's strength was replenished and future crops were secured. By drawing new life from humanity, the god's vitality, at least for the coming summer, was assured.

In these examples we see a pattern. Throughout history, people have often worshiped gods whose temperaments, passions, and shortcomings were as human as their own. There has been a tendency to project upon the objects of our worship that which is most real for us.

THIS PATTERN was shattered by Yahweh, the God of ancient Israel. The dynamic of a god's similarity to, and dependence upon, the people it governed was thoroughly dismantled by the God of the Hebrews. Yahweh, also the God of the present-day Christian church, came to be known to His people as the everywhere-present, all-knowing, all-powerful One who is complete in Himself.

In stark contrast to the gods of other nations, there is no record of Yahweh waiting patiently on His pedestal for His bath. There is no account of Him anticipating with hungry helplessness the arrival of His next meal, or calling for holy water to keep His chamber pure. He never had to draw from human strength to fight personal fatigue, or borrow enough energy to survive an approaching summer.

Instead, Israel was subject to a much different interaction with her God than that experienced by any of her neighbors. As worshipers of an invisible God, Israel was not allowed (nor actually able) to define in any chiseled, visible way His shape and substance. As the follower of One who moves about at will, she was allowed no stationary stone image by which to track and capture Him. Yahweh was utterly "other" and this His people understood. In fact, whenever Israel lapsed in this understanding, succumbed to foreign influence, and approached Yahweh as other nations approached their gods, He would throw off her efforts with disgust:

> "Listen, my people, I will speak;
> Israel, I will testify against you;
> God, your God, am I.
> I need no bullock from your house,
> no goats from your fold.
> For every animal of the forest is mine,
> beasts by the thousands on my mountains.
> I know every bird of the heavens;
> the creatures of the field belong to me.
> *Were I hungry, I would not tell you,*
> *for mine is the world and all that fills it.*
> *Do I eat the flesh of bulls*
> *or drink the blood of goats?"*
>
> —Psalm 50:7, 9–13 NAB *(italics mine)*

> To whom can you liken me as an equal?
> says the Holy One.

Do you not know
  or have you not heard?
The Lord is the eternal God,
  creator of the ends of the earth.
He does not faint nor grow weary,
  and his knowledge is beyond scrutiny.
He gives strength to the fainting;
  for the weak he makes vigor abound.
Though young men faint and grow weary,
  and youths stagger and fall,
They that hope in the Lord will renew their
    strength,
  they will soar as with eagles' wings;
They will run and not grow weary,
  walk and not grow faint.

—Isaiah 40:25, 28–31 NAB *(italics mine)*

In these passages God sets Himself apart from the gods of Israel's neighbors. Though surrounded by societies whose deities required constant upkeep, Israel's God was not weak and dependent, but mighty and strong. He was not intellectually fragile, but the One whose knowledge was "beyond scrutiny." He knew "every bird of the heavens"; "every animal of the forest" belonged to Him.

WHEN WE as Christians seek to minister to this same God, we should not imagine that we can meet His needs, for He doesn't have any. Neither should we, like the Babylonians, try to minister to Him in a way that reflects our nature instead of His.

This can be an area of struggle for many of us—it has been for me. It's not unusual for me, like worshipers of long ago, to see God through the filter of my own finite nature. Unless clearly focused on Him as He is presented in the Bible, I tend to view God through the lens of my own human frailty.

In many subtle ways I superimpose upon God what is true for me and then, because of who *I* am, I have trouble trusting Him. I transfer to God's account my own failing resources, then worry that I will "use up" His love or deplete His provision. Instead of trusting His welcome and approaching Him boldly, I inch forward cautiously, with uneasy, tentative steps. My own narrowness of soul hides the breadth of His heart, and I fear causing Him just enough trouble to outdistance His grace. In short, I expect to find God as fragile in His faithfulness as I am, and as ready to cut off communication as His comfort might require.

Over the years, however, this has proved to be a false set of fears. It is not an idol that I worship, but the living God! It is not a brittle, breakable stone image, but the living Rock—the Rock of Ages—who is my refuge! Time and again, God has shown me that it is not my own nature but the nature of His Son Jesus, the precious Cornerstone, upon whose substance is built my ministry to Him.

Jesus, our marvelous High Priest, can "sympathize with our weaknesses," but not be defined by them. He "who has been tempted in all things as we are, yet without sin" (Heb. 4:15) has redeemed me. Far from revitalizing Him with the gift of my life, I have become the beneficiary of His (John 6:35). Now I, in communion with millions of fellow Christians, drink of *His* blood, eat of *His* flesh, and draw from Him the strength to embrace, not just another summer, but eternity.

So it is that, as Christians, we take our life from God, never He from us. We draw our strength from the vast reservoir of His supply, and from this supply we too become strong.

Through the blood of Jesus we have become the sons of God, and from the security of this relationship we begin to respond to God with confidence. Our heavenly Father has genetically reproduced in us all that is necessary for priestly ministry to Him; He has, through the person of His Son Jesus, given to us the essence of His very own nature.

WHAT, THEN, is this new nature? What are some of the defining characteristics of this God whose life we now share? For an answer we turn to the Bible. Its pages do more than describe God's actions; they record His involvement with mankind and reveal *who* He is. Statements that come to us in the declarative "God is" format clarify those characteristics that make up the essence of the God that we serve. As we seek to minister to God, three such statements become essential to our understanding:

1. "Holy is the Lord God" (Rev. 4:8).
2. "God is love" (1 John 4:16).
3. "Our God is a consuming fire" (Heb. 12:29).

These three statements are important because they tell us what to expect when we come before the living God.

The first one tells us that our God is holy. Because He is holy, our ministry to Him must be the same; it must function through the righteousness of Jesus Christ alone. It can have no presumptuous self-reliance, for we must remain completely dependent upon Him even as we seek to minister to Him. It can have no sinful, self-serving aspect, for it must be genuinely centered on God. The life of Jesus in us makes it possible for our ministry to God to be holy, even as He is holy.

Secondly, we recognize that the nature of our God is love. He is guided by His affections and thoroughly resolved to pursue relationship with us. The relationship He desires is one of love, not of mutual need. The Scriptures indicate that God seeks us because He *loves* us, not because He needs us. John 3:16 does not say, "For God so needed the world, that He sent His only begotten Son." Neither does it say, "For the world so needed God, that He sent His only Son." Instead it says, "For God so *loved* the world, that He gave His only begotten Son, that whoever believes in Him should not perish, but have eternal life."

God's motivation for interaction with mankind has always been love, not need. When we approach God in ministry then, we align ourselves with the love-standard He has set. We receive God's love for us and, in an act of genuine reciprocation, respond out of our love for Him.

Thirdly, we recognize that our God is a consuming fire. This means that everything He touches is in some way branded by His passionate nature. His fire is part and parcel of all that He is—the flaming hallmark of all that He does. He is never passive or apathetic. His holiness is not a static, doctrinal theory, but an unrelenting, searing truth. His love is more than the soft, warm hug with which He soothes our pain; it is also the arresting, fiery embrace with which He cleans and cauterizes the deepest of our wounds.

God is never coolly disinterested in the world He created. He is not mechanical in His actions, but profoundly passionate about everything that has secured His devotion. If, therefore, we want to minister effectively to this passionate God, we approach Him in like manner. We allow the full measure of our own passion to express itself as we respond to Him; we pursue Him boldly, intentionally. Long after our needs have been met, we come, extending to Him the reach of our heart—stretching toward His.

As we do this, as the undiluted intensity of our devotion draws us into the presence of God, we find that the very things that move the heart of God begin to move our hearts as well. No longer are we preoccupied by our own thoughts, but by His. We are not mesmerized by the sound of our own voice speaking our own words, but by His voice speaking His Word. Ultimately, as we partake not only of God's tenderness and patience but of His strength and fire, we begin to express the very life of Jesus Christ. More and more clearly we hear The Music of the Godhead and participate with Jesus in the love that He has for His Father.

As those who carry within us the very nature of Jesus Christ, we can come to God just as Jesus did. We can approach boldly and with great confidence. This is the key. This is the truth which unlocks for us all that is pleasing and priestly in our ministry to God. It is the willingness to believe we were created to carry His *heart*, not just His bath water, that secures our ministry to Him.

THIS, THEN, is how we minister to God. We come to Him as Jesus did—not as cringing servants but as loving sons and daughters. We come not just as those who have been commissioned to do His sovereign will, but as those who *commune* with Him as we obey. As His children we bend our backs to the earthly tasks before us, but we are yoked by love, not duty, to the Lord of our labor.

I remember the time in my life when this truth became most real to me. For months I had been dodging a project that I knew God wanted me to do. As I faced the risks involved, I became increasingly anxious and afraid. Finally, in a fit of frustration, I cried out, "Lord, I want to do what You've asked of me but I just don't know how. I feel alone and afraid. I'm afraid of failing You. And, I'm afraid of being alone as I try to please You."

During the months of postponement and worry, I had gotten the notion that God wanted me to accomplish something for Him on my own, with my own meager resources and in my own feeble strength. Though I knew better, I began to see Him as a distant, demanding boss who had assigned a job too hard for me to do.

In response to my fear, God spoke these words to my heart: "Child, I understand. You don't want to do this alone—and neither do I. It's fellowship I'm interested in, not just results. I don't need you. In fact, it would be easier for Me not to use you, but I want you with Me as this thing unfolds and develops. You don't have to bring special skill or expertise; just bring your heart. I want the force of your own passion for this project to mix with Mine, and out of that will come something that ministers to Me."

It was at this point that I began to glimpse what really matters to God. Relationship matters; interaction matters. God is not lonely. He is not needy. There is nothing about Him that requires "help" from outside of Himself. Nevertheless, like any true father, He desires fellowship with His sons and daughters. Though He is in no way dependent upon us, He passionately pursues relationship with us. Love and interaction are a function of *who* God is, not His means of accomplishing a desired end.

Here on earth, relationships (for all of the discussion and interest they generate) are often the means to an end for us; they are what we "have" while we "do" something else. We are surrounded by relationships, but driven by accomplishment.

God is the opposite. Though surrounded by His accomplishments, He has given Himself to relationship. Though not in need of interaction, He has chosen to pursue it. For God, fellowship *is* the goal.

Many a mother knows the dilemma of having her four-year-old offer to help set the table for important guests. Not wanting to offend, she weighs the odds. Will it be worth it? By the time all the spoons are painstakingly placed upside down on the wrong side of each plate and the napkins have been carefully crumpled, by the time she's swept up the spilled sugar and rescued the butter dish from the dog, will it be worth the time and effort? The goal is to have a decent-looking table. Will it even come close?

For God, these situations are fairly clear-cut. There's no one He's trying to impress; there are no other, more important guests—there are only four-year-olds. They are the guests and they are the goal. The table is being set for a meal with them, not in preparation for some other group of more important people.

Every mother who's risked it knows the richness of the meal that follows the help of a child. In spite of how the table looks, regardless of how many things fell to the floor or spilled in the process, the meal they share is more than food—it is fellowship.

Something has passed between them. They have stumbled through a process together, a process the mom could have accomplished more efficiently and with less mess if she had worked alone. But the child was drawn to her side and allowed to touch the things that are precious to her. Little four-year-old smudges mark her favorite pieces of crystal and china. Large four-year-old spills decorate an otherwise spotless tablecloth. Smudging, smiling, and spilling, her child has entered her world and carried the things of her heart.

In this we see a small glimpse of the nature of God's heart toward us. We begin to see that it is not just the quality of our stewardship, but the confidence with which we embrace sonship, that touches Him.

If we insist on seeing ourselves only as servants, our labor will be heavy, taxing, and far from Him. If we trust in our ability to function for God more than we do in His desire to live through us, we will be consumed by fear of failure. If, however, we take God at His word and approach Him as His much-loved children, the entire arena of intimate interaction opens to us.

If we come as beloved sons and daughters, the vast expanse of this place that is "the priesthood of the believer" becomes ours to explore. It is, after all, the priesthood of the *believer*—those who believe God's word and His welcome—that we enter.

As ministers to God in this place, as His children, we are given access to the secrets of His heart and made welcome to the wisdom of His written Word. He speaks and we are trusted with His thoughts. He charts a course and we are called to His side as those in whom He delights to confide.

Drawn ever more deeply into His confidence, we collaborate with God in His love for the world. We share with Him in His endless compassions and participate with His heart as he formulates His will. Confident of His interest, we speak. Convinced of His pleasure, we act. With complete God-centered abandon we "draw near with confidence to the throne of grace" (Heb. 4:16), letting our "requests be made known to God" (Phil. 4:6), knowing that in the marvelous, irresistible strategy of His love,

God has every intention of honoring our desires as He accomplishes His own.

IN PART THREE of this book we will look more closely at how God leads us into a posture of sonship as we walk with Him. We will see that it is God Himself who helps us choose more than just servanthood, and how it is by His hand that we are brought into fullness of fellowship.

Before that, however, I want to look at the nature of the fellowship we have been called to enter. In part two we will talk about intimacy with God, why we often find it so intimidating, and how we should respond in the face of our fear.

PART II

The Furnace of Fellowship

Now Mount Sinai was all in smoke because the Lord descended upon it in fire; and its smoke ascended like the smoke of a furnace, and the whole mountain quaked violently.

—Exodus 19:18

5

THE FURNACE OF FELLOWSHIP

Jesus is our example in all things pertaining to God. His interaction with His Father is our truest model of ministry to God. To become effective in ministry to God's heart, therefore, we must become like Jesus. This we do, not simply by approximating and reproducing the actions of Jesus toward His Father, but by partaking of the very life that He has with His Father.

IF I SHUT my eyes and think back, I can remember the rare and wonderful campfires of my childhood. I can remember the feel of a cool, clear autumn evening, the smell of September smoke and the general hubbub of activity as our family dragged lawn chairs into position around a stack of dry, ready logs.

Our preparations were always rustic and simple. The remains of our picnic supper were stashed in the cooler, sticky fingers rinsed at the pump, then we kids headed off for one final tromp through the Illinois woods looking for bits of dry bark and tinder.

Finally, after dad coaxed a small flicker into mature flame, we'd settle ourselves for the evening ahead. Faces hot, backs cold, we stared for hours into the brightness of the blaze. Huddled safely within the warm ring of the night fire, we felt protected from the darkness, shut in with the sweet, heavy scent of a dying summer.

Endless cycles of conversation passed between us with no one feeling the need to see faces, check expressions, or meet each other's eyes. None of us seemed to notice each other's movements at all. We were watching the fire. Only the fire seemed to move. Only the random gestures of the flame's fingers held our attention, and we sat thoroughly entertained by their every darting movement, mesmerized by every shift of the glowing coals.

Together we watched and waited expectantly. As time passed and the flames descended slowly, deeply into the logs, a small, throbbing structure would appear. As the wood was carved and hollowed out by the heat, an inner chamber of liquid fire formed. What was once a pile of dry timber had become a searing sanctuary of light; something in there was alive! We could all sense it. The white-hot center of the fire was surging, pounding—we could see its pulse!

Sticks were sent in to explore. As the conversation circled around and around, we jabbed and poked among the inner embers of the fire. Probing the places of intense heat, we tried, with our long wooden fingers, to feel the pulsating heart before us. We traced the great glowing arteries, touching, testing, searching for the source of life within.

Finally, with our eyes dry from the heat, our bodies stiff, and our stories told, we prepared to leave. The sticks were then pulled from the fire, their ends red and glowing and alive.

JESUS HAS been seen as the cozy, approachable flame that welcomes us. We have settled ourselves near the gentle warmth of Him and, like squatters gathered around a campfire, have watched His every movement with interest.

Sitting near Him in the light of His love, we have found our peace. Here we have talked freely, shared openly, and explored the inner working of His ways. We have felt at ease as we probed the mysterious pathways of His power and pondered the endless nuances of His words. Feeling protected and safe, we have sent our "sticks" into His presence and have rested securely in the knowledge that they will return to us bright with borrowed fire. We have grown well content with the diffused light of our Lord and the steady comfort that His presence provides.

But we forget. We lose track of who He is and where He comes from. We think we are safe, but we are not.

Jesus comes from the flaming furnace of a raging, intimate fellowship and there is nothing entirely "safe" here. There never has been. Jesus is the very substance of a love so full and fiery that even heaven must work to withstand the force of it. Even the angels fail to find a leisurely, relaxed position with which to greet the exposed glory of the triune God (Isa. 6:2).

So it is that, on occasion, our gentle Jesus chooses to surprise us. Sometimes when we least expect it (perhaps we're postured for a time of warm, chatty prayer or drowsy, uneventful worship), He rips past the protective space between us and, like a night-fire gone awry, stings us with eternity. He comes close, really close, and we feel the searing heat of a presence too bright, too beautiful, to be endured quietly.

Pulling back, we search for the more predictable Jesus that we trust—the Jesus who warms but never burns, whose light comforts but never blinds. We search for the Jesus of our past experience, the "perfect gentleman" who patiently encouraged our troubled heart, unscrambled our tangled thoughts, and beckoned rather than pushed us past the points of our resistance.

We search, but He is gone; in His place is something not entirely gentlemanly or mindful of our boundaries. Having unwittingly lost track of our quiet campfire, we now face a forest fire instead. In place of our cozy puddle of warmth, instead of our snug talking-spot, there before us is a massive, roaring tower of flame! All of our warning systems go into effect; all of our alarms start to scream, and instantly we know we are in danger. Suddenly we are facing the grand, unfathomable passion of God—the glorious *inferno* of intimacy that is the Godhead—Christ's home.

Somehow, without anyone tipping us off, we know that this overpowering presence would not yield to idle exploration. Instinctively, we sense that no poking, probing stick would come back to us glowing. It would not come back at all, and we stand shaken before the force of such a fellowship.

THE Scriptures tell us that God is living, eternal, and mysterious in all His ways. He is uncreated, self-existent, with no beginning and no end. He is simultaneously Three and One. Each person, each expression of the Godhead carries within Himself the full attributes of God. Each one is God; One God . . . not three. The Father, Son, and Holy Spirit have been together always. Never have they not been one and the same God.

Nothing from outside of God in any way holds Him together. Nothing binds Him to Himself but Himself. There are no forces at work to confine or restrain Him, for He transcends all the natural laws that affect us. He exists far beyond all boundaries that give shape and form to our lives. Everything that is constraining to God is done from within.

"Within," there is a covenant of communion, a fellowship of profound and passionate faithfulness. There is nothing passive here. This is a fiery blast-furnace of intimacy and love. Only to the demands of their own internal covenant, only to the force of their own sovereign celebration, do the members of the Godhead submit, and nothing external is allowed to violate their union. They are ever One, never separately three.

A fierce fidelity stands guard over this churning crossfire of mutual love and devotion. Absolute allegiance shoots like liquid fire throughout the Godhead. Nothing so interests the Son as the glory of the Father. Nothing is more important to the Father than the love of His Son, and nothing so satisfies the Spirit as the glorious communion between them. A piercing, searing symmetry of honor and adoration penetrates the heart of each member, and there is an eternal fusion of fellowship.

So ferocious is this fellowship, so fluid is this fiery exchange, so *terrifying* is the beauty of this interaction, that no mortal can see it and live. No one, uninvited, can approach the vortex of their virtue and survive. No one, unshielded, can safely witness the blinding dimensions of this devotion, for nothing in heaven or on the earth is allowed to interfere with this intimacy; nothing carrying the scent of "strange fire" is tolerated in the midst of this white-hot holiness.

So compelling is the power of this union that God need only speak His own name, "I AM," and all of time is swallowed by eternity. We are time-bound. We are born, we age, and we die. He who transcends all time and space simply "is." He is eternally the same; He is One. "Hear, O Israel! The Lord is our God, the Lord is one!" (Deut. 6:4).

It is out of this intimate union that the Spirit of Jesus, the Holy Spirit, comes to the earth. He comes not just as a spark thrown from the eternal furnace.

He is not resident with us as a splintered-off subsection of God, disengaged and sent down to represent God. He *is* God. The very fullness of the Godhead dwells in Him, and when we open ourselves to the love of Jesus, it is *we* who are probed and poked. It is *our* heart that is searched and explored. We are cleansed and made ready for the consuming fire that cannot be kept a safe stick's-distance away. We are prepared for the One whose love must ultimately brand us from within.

THROUGHOUT the days of Israel's patriarchs, priests, and kings, God often represented Himself to the earth in the form of fire. He came as a flaming torch to Abram, a fiery bush to Moses, and as a pillar of flame to the nation of Israel as they fled Egypt. He fell many times as a consuming fire of judgment upon the enemies of Israel, and received with consecrating fire the sacrifices of David, Solomon, and Elijah.

The last recorded manifestation of God's fire on earth took place shortly after Jesus' return to His Father. Tongues of fire appeared on the heads of the disciples on a day known as Pentecost (Acts 2:1–4). This is the day that the Holy Spirit came publicly and with power to take up residence within mankind. That being the case, it seems that God should have sent doves to rest on the heads of each of the disciples to symbolize their infilling. He did not. He sent fire.

God was determined that the earth should perceive not just that the Spirit had come—but all that the Spirit brought with Him when He came, for

He did not come alone. He brought the same surging celebration that was present at creation, the same fiery exchange of passion that has marked the inner life of the Godhead throughout the ages. Carrying the flaming insignia of an eternal, unquenchable love, the Holy Spirit brought the towering holiness of Yahweh and the penetrating presence of Jesus—to live within us.

The Spirit came as fire and as a mighty, rushing wind, ushering in the age of our adoption—the age of God as "our" Father (Gal. 4:6–7). Through the death and resurrection of His Son Jesus, all who believed were now made sons and daughters, partakers of the flame, joint heirs of the fire of His fellowship.

There in Jerusalem, in the shadow of the temple, a greater temple was formed—one made of human hearts (1 Cor. 6:19; John 4:21–24). There, in the shadow of the Law, a greater law was given—the law of everlasting love (John 13:34). God would no longer meet with mankind only amid the smoke and stone of ritual sacrifice. No longer would His favor fall merely on the keeping of feasts and the shearing of foreskin. All things had finally been claimed by the covenant "within"; all citizens were now subject to a higher court than Caesar; all authority was now held by One with nail prints in His hands.

The tongues of fire were God's divine declaration of intent. They were the searing seal of His new covenant. From this day forward, the God of Israel would inhabit every circumcised heart and dwell forever with any who lived within the law of His love. He would now tabernacle in the redeemed hearts of men and women throughout the earth, and commune with any who worshiped Him in spirit and in truth (1 Cor. 3:16; John 4:23). He would, from this time on, make the temples of their bodies His new meeting place and fall again with holy fire upon each *living* sacrifice.

6

The Fear of Fellowship

Though most of us have sensed the greater call of God on our lives, we are often afraid of moving forward into a more intimate fellowship with Him. Even though there are countless scriptural assurances of our welcome, we struggle with fear of the very thing we were created for.

MANY OF US who make up the church, the body of Christ on earth, have scratched out an existence for ourselves between two fears. We have set up camp in what seemed like a safe place—a demilitarized zone. Wedged between opposing realities, we have formed a third world, not in the grave but not in God's glory, not back in Egypt but not in Canaan, either. For years we have peered from the shadows, but still stand shy of life—not in heaven, not in hell. All in all, it is a strangely protective purgatory we have found for ourselves—a dubious sort of safety that endeavors to shield us from the grip of the enemy and the presence of God.

I know a much-loved little boy who, when he was three, would pray in tiny, simple, fresh words to a God he was just beginning to know. By the age of five, however, he was praying tight, choppy prayers, always using the same words: "Dear God, thank you for this good day and this good night. Please take care of daddy and mommy. Please don't let any robbers come tonight. Please don't let the house catch on fire. Please help me not to have bad dreams. Amen."

This fairly direct set of requests could take up to five minutes if, for some reason, he faltered over the exact wording or forgot one of the crucial elements. His little face would scrunch up, his tiny fingers would press hard into a proper, sweaty prayer-fist, and he would struggle to get everything said so that nothing bad would happen.

As his parents, it hurt us to watch this scene. My husband and I wrestled with our desire to break into "the system" and put him in touch with the real God, the living God, so that he could pray real, living prayers. Even so, we knew that only God could truly reveal Himself to the heart of a five-year-old.

Somehow, in two brief years of consciously interacting with God, ritual had already emerged. Where had it come from? At what point did the formula become safe and the real God fade into fear? When did the past take over the present? This prayer was the true expression of his little heart the first time he prayed it, maybe even the first few times. But now it had become a well-worn lucky charm, an incantation.

More difficult still was the peace that would settle in as soon as the ritual was successfully completed. The fidgeting would stop, his face would relax, his duty was done. It's not that he didn't believe in God. He most fervently did. That's why it was so important to get it right. He felt that the things of God, those things that already had meaning, had to be offered again and again.

MANY OF US hide a five-year-old deep inside our adulthood. We feel compelled to return to that time when we sensed a genuine communication with God, then try to repeat it verbatim. That time when we really felt His presence becomes a prototype for all future interaction, and we are sure of His pleasure only as we repeat the performances of the past. Ritual, though often the second and third generation of an experience that was once very real, can become our refuge from current communion with God.

It takes courage to live in the present with a fiery God of intimacy and adventure, especially when His primary agenda is to form the full expression of His Son in us. We try to stay pliable in the hand of God but fear what He may ultimately require of us. We see the necessity and inevitability of change but feel secure only if we get to regulate the amount of pressure we're under in the process. We have every intention of cooperating with God as He moves us toward maturity, but end up protecting ourselves instead.

IT HAS NOT always been this way. As individuals we haven't always been so tentative in our approach to God. We can remember that even though our first steps toward Jesus required great faith, we responded well. We trusted Him. We came simply, unfalteringly, into the stream that separated us from God, and there we willingly died to our sin. In this baptism of our souls, we died to our old nature and were given a new one.

Gradually, however, as our faces broke the surface of the stream, as we shook the water from our eyes and gazed ahead, we recognized with some shock the requirements of our new life. Startled, we surveyed the fullness of the fellowship that awaited on the far shore.

We had believed, accepted, and acted upon this truth: To live with God, we must die to ourselves (Rom. 6:4, 11). We knew that to be born again we had to embrace not only the cradle but the cross; the Bible says so. This, however, is only half the story. The Scriptures also tell us that if we follow Jesus into death we must follow Him into His resurrection life as well (Rom. 6:5–7). *If* we die, then we *must* live again. God requires it. In fact, God not only requires new life, He provides for it. In the Father's plan, resurrection always follows the faith that the cross entails.

So, if we wade into the stream, we must wade back out on the other side—it is not enough to tread water at the spot of our salvation, caught in the crosscurrent of the past and the future. We are not meant to swim endless circles around the site of our surrender, remembering only the glory of that moment. We are called to cross over into fellowship with God, into the ongoing glory of His presence.

We have been called and we must respond, but it is here that fear often wells up within us, for it seems a dangerous resurrection that we face. We are still flesh and blood and, as desperately as we want to be with God, we instinctively protect ourselves from the white-hot intimacy that is now our new home. Our arms go up, not in surrender but as a shield, not in welcome but withdrawal.

Even though this is what Christ died to give us, even though this blinding Light is the other side of our salvation, we cover our eyes and our expectations. We back away.

Like hunted animals scratching at a wall, we search for the crack between death and resurrection, hoping for entrance into a sliver of safety—a crevice of cooler, softer light. With fear as our guide, we scramble for a protected place somewhere between the silence of the tomb and the sound of God's voice.

The intensity of God's devotion is more than we bargained for. The ultimate tone of His intentions is unnerving. We feel pushed from behind to embrace things we don't understand.

We knew Jesus would be our friend, our companion, our eternal habitation, but we didn't expect to be His. We knew that God had a "wonderful plan for our lives"; we just didn't understand that He had a wonderful plan for His Son as well. We understood that Christ carried the weight of our sin in His mortal body, but we never counted on carrying the weight of His glory in ours!

We wanted a discreet, civilized agreement with God, not the crucible of a covenant. We wanted to be with Him in heaven someday; now He's rushing heaven into our hearts—to dwell in us. We wanted to have friendly fellowship, but certainly not fusion, nothing as confining as "oneness"! We wanted to minister *for* Him, not *to* Him. We wanted a method, not a marriage.

But again, the Scriptures are clear. It is marriage that we're headed for (Rev. 19:7). Corporately we are the bride of Christ, not His maid. There will be no stiff, staid communion between us. There will be no safe, isolated servanthood. A vow has been made, His word has been given, and we have given ours.

IT IS HERE that we recognize one of Christianity's central, over-arching truths: God has never given us a choice about the *nature* of what we have been called to enter. The only choice we have is whether or not to go in. Our God is truly a consuming fire, and this fire will not be curtailed simply for our comfort. His blinding, blazing light was evident long before the age began, and it will not be darkened or diffused merely to save our sight. Our God will not be less than who He is.

So, we have a choice. We can enter the place of His dwelling, or we can stand clear. We can proceed in faith or we can falter; but we must know this—there is no heaven but this one.

There is no "safe" mist-covered neutrality waiting for us on the other side. There is no cool, private accommodation somewhere in our future, for the fire of intimacy is the very nature of the Father's house. God's heaven is where He is and there is no buffer zone between. There is no way for us to stand on the outside of intimacy and still know salvation. We either face the fire of fellowship with Him or the fire of isolation and hell without Him (John 15:4–6).

It is not enough to die to sin; we must live to Christ. It is not enough to wake from the sleep of the grave; we must step forth and shed all the trappings of death. We must strip ourselves free of soiled grave-clothes. Throwing off guilt, we must embrace grace; throwing off comfort, we must pursue Christ. He must have our first loyalty, our first allegiance. His heart must be our first ministry, and the demands of our other ministries must wait!

IF IT IS, therefore, truly God that we desire, then it is the furnace of fellowship that we must enter. If it is the name of Christ that we wear, then He is the One we must follow. As *Christ*ians, we go where Jesus goes—deep into the dwelling place of the Father.

This call to oneness and intimacy is binding for every true believer. For us it is the only choice. Never has walking in the fire of God's presence been an optional activity for those who genuinely want to follow Jesus. Never has the pursuit of God's manifest glory been reserved only for those who want the "advanced course" in Christianity. It is all He has offered to any of us. There is no easier way. There is no middle ground for us—for there is no life in limbo nor resurrection power in the netherworld of neutrality.

7

PARTAKERS OF THE FLAME

What, then, can be said? Must we enter God's presence, this frightening arena of intimacy and oneness? Yes, we must. Is it really necessary that we go there, that we pursue this "dangerous" destination? Yes, it is. For our God has called us by name . . . into His life . . . into His glory. He loves us and wants us with Him where He is (John 17:20–24).

WE CANNOT truly enter the presence of Jesus without His presence entering and changing us. We cannot genuinely know Him without the brand of that knowledge marking our hearts forever.

As the influence of Jesus becomes more and more active within us, we begin to resonate with the same fluid, fiery exchange that accompanies every interaction of the Godhead.

It is into the ever-deepening dimensions of this intimacy that we have been called. It is an ever-clearer image of this oneness, this glory, this *music*, that we have been commissioned to carry. Caught in the whirling centrifuge of loving conversation between the Father and the Son, we have become communicators with the living God. Under the influence of the Holy Spirit we have become participants in the great exchange-of-hearts that spans all of time and space. Hearing the cry of God's heart and responding with the cry of our own, we enter the lightning-like volley of the Godhead's own passionate exchange.

We enter this exchange not as equals with God but as ministers to Him. We participate as those who have had this place prepared for them by the blood of Jesus Christ. We come before the face of this intimacy knowing full well that, except for the protection of Christ's righteousness, we would be instantly destroyed (John 14:6).

Covered in Christ, however, we are not destroyed. Instead, we live! Actually, we live "abundantly beyond all that we ask or think" (Eph. 3:20), for we have been seated "with Him [Christ] in the heavenly places" (Eph. 2:6). Clothed in the virtue of Jesus Christ, we are escorted into the very arena of God's own oneness (John 17:20–21).

We are not kept at a distance. We are not removed to a more respectful, remote location.

There is no separate, roped-off corner of the cosmos from which we are to merely watch in wonder and observe in amazement. We have been called *in*!

The gospel of John reflects nothing forced or begrudging in Christ's manner as He cried out, "Father, I desire that they also, whom Thou hast given Me, be with Me where I am, in order that they may behold My glory" (John 17:24).

We have been called in "to behold" Christ's glory. The Greek word used here for "behold" is *theoreo* and, as used in this passage, it means to "experience in the sense of partaking."[1] We partake of Christ's life and His glory. As with all followers of Jesus throughout the ages, we have been called into the same exchange of fire that Christ has always known!

Never had the angelic hosts witnessed such a gift of love and mercy. Never, prior to the cross, had heaven seen anything like it. For thousands of years they watched each stage of this drama unfold. They watched as their Master, the God of all power, pursued His creation. Incredulous, they witnessed the price of His pursuit. At Calvary they saw the Battle and the Blood. They watched as the body of Jesus was torn on the cross and the veil in the temple was torn in two, and they knew then that we, wretched, beloved humanity, would always be the subject of their greatest amazement.

Throughout the ages, the story would be told again and again. The wonder of heaven would ever

---

[1] Zodhiates, Spiros, ed. *The Hebrew-Greek Key Study Bible* (Chattanooga, Tennessee: AMG Publ., 1990), p. 1841.

increase: "What is man, that Thou dost take thought of him? And the son of man, that Thou dost care for him? Yet Thou hast made him a little lower than God, and dost crown him with glory and majesty!" (Ps. 8:4–5).

No longer do we as mortal men and women need to be kept safe from the presence of God. No longer do we need to cringe in self-protection, for now we are welcomed with great joy and celebration. Jesus said it best in His final declaration to a bewildered world: "It is finished!" The separation is over. The kingdom of heaven is at hand.

So it is that now we come boldly into our communion and walk with assurance into the fire of this fellowship, for Christ has gone before us. No longer do we offer to God our cautious compliance nor bring to Him the fragile praise of a fearful heart. No longer do we rush from His presence into our busy-ness, nor assume a stance of remote interaction.

Instead, carrying within us the confidence and covering of the cross, we joyfully enter the great, ageless exchange-of-hearts. We are joint heirs with Jesus in the love of His Father! We drink from His cup and partake of His portion! Bequeathed the treasures of His kingdom and afforded the full rights of His righteousness, the furnace of His fellowship has become our new home!

PART III

The Way In

But you will be called
the priests of the Lord;
You will be spoken of as
ministers of our God.

—Isaiah 61:6

8

THE WAY IN

As exciting and terrifying as the notion is, it seems a bit simplistic to speak in terms of a "furnace of fellowship." It seems naive to suggest that all we have to do is face our fear, pack our bags and start off "into the fire."

Though oddly childlike, it's true. There really is a God of intense intimacy and love who wants our fellowship. The Bible says so. There really are fears to be faced, preparations to be made, and a road that each of us must travel.

BECAUSE we are finite beings, we tend to be linear in our thinking and consecutive in our movements. We start and finish a book, begin and end our workday, and look "forward to" and "back on" any given event.

Time and production have become the measurements of our progress. As we assess the success of our day, we think in terms of having had enough time to accomplish our tasks or having advanced near enough to our goals to warrant our rest.

We are process oriented. If we sculpt or paint, choreograph or compose, we move through the many stages that such creativity requires. When we travel or move from one place to another, we define a point of departure and focus on a point of arrival. We proceed in increments of time and space, always viewing the journey in light of our destination.

We would, however, be naive to think that God is as we are. I believe He is much more simultaneous and circular, perhaps even spherical, in His actions. He does not search for a beginning and an end to something; He *is* the beginning and the end. He does not examine an event from a time/space ratio, for He exists far outside of time and His purposes can be accomplished even as they are conceived. They do not have to happen in time and space before they are real to Him.

God does not, as far as we know, have a production schedule that He must meet. He does not require of Himself "two new galaxies before noon" or to "complete a new firmament by nightfall." That would be absurd. He *is* the noon . . . He *is* the nightfall. He carries the hourglass; we are the ones who must live within it. He speaks, and stars appear; with a word, worlds are formed. God is not trapped in time and process as we are.

How, then, can we approach Him except that He help us? How can the finite interact with the infinite apart from assistance? We have been curtailed by sin. We move one step at a time. We must travel to places . . . even to the places of God's heart.

Paradoxically, we find ourselves needing to walk *with* God into the very presence *of* God. He is not subject to process, but since we are, He is careful to lead us. He reaches out to us, takes us by the hand, and moves us step-by-step into the furnace of fellowship.

God is good at this. He is patient. For all the fire of His holy nature, He is still a father with a father's heart, and He has taught many children how to walk. He has drawn entire nations along by the hand and He will help us if we let Him.

OUR FIRST STEP toward the furnace of fellowship is a very simple one. In other, more elaborate religious systems, it would seem too basic, too elementary, to be noticed. We, however, must notice and discuss it here because it is the key to everything that will come after.

It is this: We make a response to God. That is all. The quality of our response does not initially matter. How *well* we do what we do is, at first, of little or no importance. Whether we react to God with some magnificent gesture of devotion or a minute, almost imperceptible, flicker of faith is hardly the issue. That we make a genuine, purposeful response to God is, however, essential.

It is essential because we are drawn into the furnace of fellowship by a process of communicating with God. He speaks and we respond. He then responds to our response and soon the silken cord of conversation takes shape between us. It is to this cord that we cling as we make our way into the place of His presence.

Communion with God in the furnace of fellowship begins with conversation with Jesus here and now. In fact, throughout the Scriptures and the history of the church, the pattern is well documented: Those who have walked with God have talked with God.

From Abraham, David, and Isaiah, to Peter, John, and Paul, from Francis of Assisi and Brother Lawrence to Hudson Taylor and Oswald Chambers, the list is long. Luther, Tyndale, Wesley, Finney, Fanny Crosby, Amy Carmichael, Andrew Murray, Watchman Nee, Livingston, Bonhoeffer, Tozer, Lewis, Moody—to be complete, the list would have to be as long as history itself. Whoever they have been, and however unknown or well publicized their lives among men, the millions of believers that have walked this earth in close communion with God have been in constant communication with Him as well. Their lives have been filled with responses to God.

I am convinced that if we were to crack open just the few lives listed above, in each and every case we would find a conversation with God. Written, sung, preached, or prayed, deep within each life would run the same silvery strands of that silken cord, leading step-by-step into the furnace of fellowship. Whether through desperate cries in times of crisis or through passionate praises and declarations of devotion, each life evolved as a series of uniquely patterned interactions with God.

Perhaps you could hear the echo of some of their words as you read through their names. "Wilt thou indeed sweep away the righteous with the wicked?" cried an anguished Abraham as he braced for the destruction of Sodom (Gen. 18:23 KJV). "My heart is steadfast, O God; . . . I will awaken the dawn! I will give thanks to Thee, O Lord, among the peoples; and I will sing praises to Thee among the nations," sang the passionate David (Ps. 108:1–3). "Woe is me, . . . I am a man of unclean lips," groaned Isaiah (Isa. 6:5); "Thou my everlasting portion," sang Fanny Crosby, "more than friend or life to me; all along my pilgrim journey, Savior, let me walk with Thee."

God, as we know, is no respecter of persons. If we want to grasp that cord and take that journey, we can. If we want to walk and talk with God, we can. In fact, if we have repented of our sins and declared faith in Jesus Christ, then we are already on the threshold of the furnace of fellowship. By genuinely embracing Jesus, God's Son, the door has been flung open and we have been called to enter.

Responding to the saving grace of Jesus is, however, only the beginning of a lifelong journey. After that, it is important that we keep taking steps toward intimacy with our Savior. This we do by continuing to respond to Him.

Daily, hourly, minute-by-minute, as we listen for God's voice and continue to answer with our own, we are drawn further and further into the great exchange-of-hearts that is our home. As we choose time and again to talk to God about all that we think and feel, He begins to weave a special, one-of-a-kind interaction with us. Through good days and bad, while facing great victory and stinging defeat, as we choose to share with our Father the real "stuff" of our hearts, He continues to reveal to us the substance of His own.

Step-by-step, conversation-by-conversation, God leads us into deeper relationship with Himself. Speaking to us from the Scriptures, He weans us from the general clamor around us and teaches us the language of His heart. He draws out the special, individual responses that are unique to each of us and, using these responses, He ushers us into ministry—ministry to Himself—out of which all other ministry must emerge.

9

THE REALM OF RESPONSE

Even as a person's first, tentative, baby steps are similar in structure to their more confident, striding adult steps, our first step toward fellowship with God is like every other step we will ever take with Him.

AS WE DISCUSSED in the last chapter, our first "baby" step toward God involves responding to Him. Because this is the first of many steps that we will take with God, and all our steps in some way mirror each other, it is important to emphasize two points. First, whatever response we make should be made *to God*. He is our focus and it is to Him that we speak. As we move forward into the furnace of fellowship, the choice we make is to respond specifically to God, not to the things around us or to the trappings of the church, not even to the "salvation message"—but to God Himself.

For all the simplicity of this thought, it is more slippery than it first appears. It is slippery because we are natural-born responders living in a stimulus-rich world. As such, we have a tendency to give away what belongs first and foremost to God. Caught in the daily whirl of interaction with those around us, we often find ourselves responding to the most urgent demands of earth before even acknowledging the call of heaven. Though we were created to respond to God, we often respond to the people and events around us instead.

This is not a new greased log we walk. It is exactly the one Eve fell from so miserably. She was created to respond to God, but chose to respond to Satan instead. Adam was not far behind; he was created to respond to God, but responded to Eve instead.

The second important element in responding to God is that it must be *our* response that we bring. When we come to God, we need to genuinely represent ourselves; we cannot push something of someone else in front of us as we make our way into His presence. We cannot borrow from another person as we try to interact with God, for it is the genuine cry of our heart that He waits to hear.

This too tends to be difficult for us. As human beings, we learn by imitation and often grow dependent upon the ways of others in the process of our spiritual education. In fact, without ever intending to, we can ride the experiential coattails of a clear-thinking pastor or passionate Bible teacher. In our desire to know more about God, we can start to depend upon someone else's relationship with Him. By imitation of another person's interaction with God, we risk preempting our own.

I remember a time when my own communication with God was interrupted by trying to imitate someone else. During my early twenties, Ann Kiemel came to the church I was attending, and in the space of one evening I was captured by the pure, childlike way she had of interacting with God. I was delighted by the candor and ease with which she responded to Him even in the midst of the large crowd that had gathered to hear her speak.

As comfortable as if she were in her own living room, Ann told stories about Jesus, sang little songs, and spread sprigs of poetry around the huge auditorium. She told us of giving flowers and God's love to people who passed by her on the big-city streets of her hometown. She sang for us the same, sweet, breathy songs that she sang to cabdrivers during traffic jams and shopkeepers on rainy days. With joy-filled spontaneity she recited the same poems that accompanied the hot-from-the-oven cookies she gave to the homeless people of her neighborhood. I was amazed by her vulnerability and warmth. She loved everyone she met. She loved hungry cats and stray dogs, burly garbagemen and crabby meter maids.

Most of all, Ann loved children. Images from the Sound of Music flooded my mind as she told of buying ice-cream cones for all the kids on her block, singing to them while they ate, captivating their hearts with stories about Jesus, then dabbing at the chocolate smudges around their smiling mouths when they were finished. I was mesmerized.

Ann was utterly charming and completely genuine. I responded longingly to her open, winsome ways and wanted God to make me just like her. Perhaps, I thought, if He would work a major miracle, I too could sing to total strangers, hug trees, and befriend abandoned animals. Perhaps, in spite of my fairly reserved personality, I could stick flowers in my hair, dance through busy intersections, and quote poetry to people on noisy street corners.

As I thought about my life, however, it seemed like a real stretch. In reviewing my fairly predictable existence, this scenario didn't seem very likely. Though I loved kids, I knew there'd be no way to control the scruffy little toughs on my block if free ice cream was involved—I'd have been trampled and left for dead in front of the concession stand. The only poem I'd heard recently was "John Brown's Body" and, with my voice, it seemed safer *not* to sing to anyone driving a car or operating heavy machinery. Ann Kiemel and I had very little in common.

Even so, I decided to try. I asked God to change me to be like her. As soon as I said the words, I knew I had made a mistake; I felt something cold move into my heart and I sensed God's displeasure. I groped around for the familiar, comfortable cord of communication that I had held onto for so many years, but for a moment my hands were empty. All I held was a mirage—a fading, unfulfilled image of someone else's time-woven interaction, and it had no substance or reality for me.

I learned something then that I have not since forgotten. I learned that God will never help me become like anyone but Jesus. He will never lend His assistance to re-creating me in any image short of that One. God is prepared to deal with an infinite number of my struggles and failures before He will agree to make me like someone else.

Far from being the effective shortcut I had imagined, praying to become like someone else is like asking God to perform a spiritual abortion. He is jealous for each of us—who we are now and who we are yet to become. Each life and each cord of communication that sustains life is of great importance to Him; He is unwilling to sever either one.

Because I have felt the blunt edge of God's resolve in this area, I know how important this issue can be. In this age of rock star heroes, image brokers, and virtual reality, Jesus alone must shape the reality of those who make up His church. It must be His image to which we are conformed and to Him that we give the true, genuine substance of our hearts.

IN THE NEXT CHAPTER we will see this more clearly. We will see that God tenaciously, patiently sojourns with us as we struggle our way into authentic, heartfelt responses. He strives with us for as long as it takes, since ultimately He desires us to come to Him *for* ourselves, *as* ourselves.

10

THE GOD WE CAN SEE

We often struggle in our attempts to respond to God because we have trouble finding Him amid all the clamor and confusion around us. One of the most acute longings of the human heart is to see for itself the God of the Scriptures. We want to see God and know that He sees us. We want to respond to Him in a way that is not distorted or obscured by our own human frailty.

SOME YEARS ago my family and I traveled to California to visit my husband's parents. During a layover in Denver, the jumbo jet we were on filled up quickly, as all around us passengers squeezed through the narrow aisles. Carry-on baggage was stuffed into the already bulging overhead compartments and jammed under every available seat. The flight was full—so full, in fact, that some families were forced to sit separately.

Just behind me sat a small two-year-old boy with his dad. Unable to get a seat in the same row, the mother had been placed quite a bit forward and to the far right. At one point during the flight, the dad lifted his son above the back of my seat so that together they could see where she was sitting. "Say hi to mommy," the father said. "See mommy? Say hi to mommy, Sam."

But Sam couldn't see mommy. His tiny eyes couldn't find her in the sea of unfamiliar heads spread out in front of him. While he looked around in growing bewilderment, his dad continued to talk and encourage. A huge fatherly hand took hold of one of his little arms and waved it in mom's direction. Over and over the words were repeated: "Say hi, Sam. See mom? Let's say hi to her! Do you see her? She's right there, now wave, tell mommy you love her." Poor Sam still didn't see his mom, so he said nothing; his arm remained limp and his face continued to register a blank, searching stare.

Finally, just as the father was ready to give up, Sam caught sight of the side of his mother's face and his tiny chest released a sudden, explosive yell. Across the entire plane everyone could hear him calling, "HI, MOMMY! . . . HI, MOM!!" His little hand began to wave furiously and his face went from blank bewilderment to frenzied joy. He saw her! He finally *saw* her amid all the unfamiliar faces, and his response was immediate and complete. Nothing had to be coaxed or persuaded out of him. In fact, he became so enthusiastic, yelling "hellos" at the top of his lungs, that the dad finally had to haul him down and distract him with a book.

I THINK we often find ourselves trying to respond to a God we don't yet "see." We know He's there but we can't find His face, so our effort at response seems hollow and forced. We tend to feel bewildered and false if we're encouraged to move through the motions and "wave" in recognition of a God we're still trying to locate.

The fact that a response is important and appropriate is no longer the issue for us. It's that we don't know where to aim it. We don't know what direction in the sea that stretches before us to send our signals. Meanwhile we're surrounded by people whose worship seems effortless and focused. Their easy enthusiasm seems to mock our own struggle for sight.

Few things are as frustrating and lonely as being in the midst of a group of excited, expressive people while not able to see what they're responding to. In college, I used to sit with a blind friend at basketball games and describe to him the games as they were being played. It was a tense arrangement for him. We were a small private college, usually locked in grim, greasy combat with another equally-small private school. Since there was no professional sportscaster, I would do my best to keep up a running commentary.

My best was pretty sketchy. Surrounded by the ricocheting screams of several hundred college kids and caught up in the general hysteria of close competition, I would sometimes forget to report on what I was seeing. Often, at the most crucial moments, I would stop talking altogether.

David would go wild. Though a patient person by nature, he could sense the suspense, hear the roar of the crowd, and smell the sweat of excitement all around him. Finally, his hands would grip my arm like a vise. "What? . . . What? . . . What's happening?!" he would yell above the crowd.

By the time I regrouped and caught him up on the action, his response was out of sync. Even if I managed to keep him current with a quick, clear description of the game, his reactions were always muted and restrained. He had none of the spontaneous, explosive responses of the other fans, since he needed to hear me to know what was going to happen next. He couldn't afford to be too loud, or he wouldn't be able to "see."

IT'S DIFFICULT for us to respond to God with fresh, fervent worship when all we have to go on is what other people are saying about Him. It's hard to be spontaneous and involved when we're straining to find Him through the filter of another person's words. Eventually, no matter how inspired the speaker, no matter how careful the commentary, we get impatient with reports of God's activity and want to see Him for ourselves. We want to throw off all the hindrances and get a glimpse of His face with our own eyes.

Like the biblical account of the little man Zaccheus (Luke 19:1–10), we stand in the back of the crowd, eyes wide open, searching, but still unable to see. There are too many other people in front of us. We can sense the excitement and hear the reaction of everyone nearby, but Jesus is still hidden from us. There are so many other "seers" that block our view, we wish He would simply clear them away. We wish Jesus would use His miraculous power to cut a path through the crowd and bring us forward, but He does not.

Instead, as with Zaccheus, Jesus waits for our desperation to reach its zenith. He waits as we scurry around the perimeter of the crowd, jumping up and down, bouncing off the bodies in front of us, growing ever more weary of our inability to see Him. Patiently, He allows time for our hunger, our desire, to escalate to the point where we are willing to do anything to get a glimpse of Him. In short, He waits for us to find a tree and climb it.

Jesus could, of course, make things easier for us, but He usually chooses not to. Instead, knowing how important this season of desperation is, He allows ample time for its full, foundational work to take shape within us. He knows that time often helps us realize the extent to which our dependence upon other people has become a blocking, hindering force. The longer we try to draw from others what only God can give, the more disillusioned we become.

Eventually we begin to realize that commentaries and reports are a God-sent encouragement, but they were never meant to sustain us. We begin to understand that, however clear someone else's view of Him may be, we cannot rely on other people in our search for Jesus. We cannot pass through them in order to find Him. We must go up. We must meet with Jesus personally and respond to Him directly.

There are countless ways to do this. Scripture indicates that, though there is only one way to find the Father—through Jesus, His Son (John 14:6)—there are innumerable ways to find the Son. Though there is only one mediator between God and men (1 Tim. 2:5), only one "door" into the furnace of fellowship (John 10:7, 9), there are as many different pathways leading up to that door as there are people wanting entrance (Matt. 11:28; John 6:37).

This is by design. There is purposely no single, approved route by which we must approach Jesus. There is no official protocol for entering His presence. No polite, civilized statements are required of us before we can say what we really mean, for it is honesty, not propriety, that interests Him. Jesus doesn't want the raw reality of our need obscured by proper etiquette; He's not interested in pretty manners that serve only as a smoke screen for our pain.

Instead, He wants each of us to come to Him in our own way, with our turmoil intact. He wants every synthetic, cosmetic device used to camouflage our heart stripped away and left behind. Everything artificial must be abandoned in our quest for Him. If we are evil, He wants us to say so. If we are hurt, He wants to hear it. If, like His disciple Peter, we have already walked with Him but betrayed our knowledge of Him somewhere along the way, He wants us to face Him once again. Real failure, real fear, real unbelief and despair are what He conquered on the cross. These cannot resist Him, but our cover-ups can.

Nothing can tempt Jesus to act in response to shaded, half-exposed realities, for He must have access by a free act of our will to the true nature of our need. He must be allowed to see the actual depth of our distress and hear the clear cry of our heart. To this He will respond. To this Jesus always responds, asking only that our desire for Him be stronger than our pride. Our desperation and desire can make a way for us into His presence.

We see this played out many times in the Bible. On one occasion a lame man was so anxious for healing that his friends climbed to the roof of the house where Jesus was staying, tore it open, and lowered him inside. Another time, while Jesus was sharing supper with a Pharisee, a sobbing prostitute defied all social restraint by falling at His feet, washing them with her tears, and drying them with her hair. Yet another time, a desolate, bleeding woman (considered to be legally "unclean" because of her illness), broke Jewish law, joined the crowd surrounding Jesus, and touched His robe.

In each case, Jesus responded. The lame man was forgiven of his sins and healed (Luke 5:25), the prostitute, forgiven of her sins and gently welcomed (Luke 7:47–50), and the bleeding woman was afforded the relief she had sought for twelve long years (Mark 5:29).

Time and again throughout the Scriptures, Jesus is shown responding to the deep desire of those who wanted to see Him for themselves and meet Him personally. The loving, active nature of His response is recorded in detail in His interaction with the hemorrhaging woman. Though He could easily have moved on without ever acknowledging her touch, Jesus stopped everything and went looking for her. He knew that He had been touched by someone's faith and He wanted to respond face-to-face. Jesus wanted to respond to the searching heart behind the grasping hand.

To the amazement of His disciples and the pushing, pressing crowd, He turned and said, "Who has touched my clothes?"

"Who touched you!?" came the reply, "You see how the crowd is pressing in upon you, and yet you ask 'Who touched me?' "

Jesus, though hemmed in on every side, knew power had gone out of Him; His eyes continued to search the faces of the crowd.

Finally, the trembling woman came forward. Greatly frightened and expecting a public rebuke, she nevertheless explained what she had done. "Daughter," said Jesus tenderly, "your faith has saved you. Go in peace and be cured of your affliction." Instead of reprimanding her for breaking Jewish law, Jesus blessed her for her great faith.

By addressing her so openly, Jesus publicly lifted from her the stigma of her sickness and the decade-long weight of her shame. By gently, intentionally, requiring that she stand out from the covering of the crowd, she was met, not with excruciating exposure but with the healing protection of His unflinching gaze.

In the simple act of responding to Jesus' call to come forward, this frightened woman stepped past the dark, tight places of her own soul into the vast arena of His acceptance and love. From this vantage point, she could see Jesus for who He really was, not as a quick-fix healer but as Messiah and Lord—not just as one who touches the body but as the One who heals the heart.

This is the beauty of coming to Jesus as we really are: we begin to see Him as He really is. While requiring that we expose the true, undisguised nature of our need, Jesus reveals the true, undiluted strength of His salvation. He is the living Word—the One who speaks as He heals. He is the God who does more than patch up the current crisis; He pursues the hidden places deep within.

This has always been His objective. Ultimately it is the cry of the human heart that Jesus seeks to meet. In order to do so, He requires that we break free of everyone else's reports and admit our own need. He asks that we leave the covering of the crowd and come to Him as we really are.

When we come to Jesus openly and without pretense, we are never rejected, never ignored. Lame men and madmen, Roman soldiers and Samaritan women, harlots, lepers, and criminals—all were loved and received; all had equal access.

IT IS the same today. Two thousand years later, Jesus' message remains passionate and clear: "Come to Me," He cries, "all who are weary and heavy-laden, and I will give you rest. Take My yoke upon you, and learn from Me, . . . For My yoke is easy, and My load is light" (Matt. 11:28–30).

Regardless of who we are or what we've done, there is still no exclusive, "correct" way to come to Jesus. All that is required is that we come in person and bring our weariness with us. There is no single, approved approach. Whether we limp in empty-handed or struggle in under a load of our own accomplishments, this one thing is necessary: It must be our own desperation that propels us forward and the draft-force of our own desire that draws us to His side.

In this way our journey is never exactly the same as anyone else's. The pressure of our own search provides us with a living record that no one else's life can duplicate. Each of us is precious to Jesus and it is often what we experience *as we seek Him* that begins to forge our individual history with Him.

I believe, in fact, that our search is as special to Jesus as it is necessary for us; for in it He celebrates those things about us that set us apart from all of His other followers. From the very onset, He nurtures the unique, even quirky, characteristics of the disciple He has called us to be.

It is with this in mind that Jesus waits patiently for us to find our "tree" and climb above the many human explanations that surround us. Jesus waits for us to move out on a limb that exposes us to His scrutiny even as it allows us an unobscured view of Him.

Then, just as with Zaccheus, everything beneath us becomes quiet. Jesus stops the chaos and confusion of the crowd and turns to look at us. He knows we're there. Now His gaze locks with ours and we see Him smile. Walking over to us, He speaks. He speaks and we respond, not to someone else's voice but to His! Not to a description of Him but to Him!

"Make haste, child, and come down," He says, "for I must stay at your house today." The force of our own reaction surprises us. We become aware of ourselves responding with all the exuberance of a small boy finding the face of his mother in a crowded airplane. Suddenly, out of nowhere, comes a voice calling, greeting, *responding* . . . and it is our own.

All at once, worship has made room for us, for Jesus has come to *our* house. He has dined with us and now we are a "responder." We have shared supper with Him, and are not hungry anymore. We have talked together and now there is nothing forced or false about our show of affection. Jesus has come to where we live, and now the wave of our hand in worship is *our* wave, *our* welcome, to the God that we can see.

11

The Reach of the Hungering Heart

"I, the Lord, am your God . . . Open your mouth wide and I will fill it." —*Psalm 81:10*

HAVING DISCUSSED our hunger to see God and the importance of expressing it, I must now address a possible concern. It has long been considered more spiritually mature to "believe without seeing." The well-known and much-quoted verse, "Blessed are they who did not see, and yet believed" (John 20:29), is often used to reward Christians who are willing to forego any sight of God. This, I believe, is a mistaken understanding of the verse and endorses an unnecessary poverty.

The context of this verse is that Jesus, upon His return from the grave, faced the skepticism of His disciple Thomas. To offset the doubts in Thomas' mind about the validity of His resurrection, Jesus showed him the nail prints in his hands and allowed him to touch the scattered, damaged flesh of each wound. This is what it took for Thomas to believe. He needed proof.

It was at this point that Jesus uttered the now-famous words praising all those who would, through the centuries, believe in His resurrection without being shown the proof of nail holes and scars.

There is a substantial difference between a person needing to see God *in order* to believe and someone wanting to see God *because* he believes. The former is a requirement of the mind, the latter is the reach of the heart.

THE SCRIPTURES indicate that the reach of the human heart has always attracted God. The eager, tiptoe stretch of a person's soul has always captured His attention—it is not a posture He ignores or denies.

Embattled old Job is one of the Bible's best examples of a stretching, questing, *reaching* heart. Though usually remembered as a forlorn figure in search of relief from his many sufferings, he was actually a strong, passionate, faith-filled man struggling for a glimpse of his God.

Job was a man who walked with God and was greatly blessed by Him long before he ever "saw" Him. So faithful a servant of the Lord was he that his reputation eventually reached hell and piqued

Satan. A rare wager was made and it was agreed that Job's trust would be tested (Job 1:6–12, 2:1–6).

Stripped of his family, health, possessions, and power, Job groped through the resulting darkness for the face of the God that he loved. Friends, convinced that his circumstances were God's judgment for hidden sin, spent long days trying to lead him to repentance.

In time, Job became weary of their help and exhausted by their admonitions. His raw, grief-stricken heart was sick with fatigue and oppressed by the endless flow of their words. Blasting past all of their well-intentioned arguments, he finally cried out in protest. Pushing against every earthly constraint, his heart broke loose, rose up, and stretched toward heaven. Job cried,

> As for me, I know that my Vindicator
> lives, . . .
> Whom I myself shall see:
> *my own eyes, not another's,* shall behold him,
> And from my flesh I shall see God;
> my inmost being is consumed with longing.
>
> —Job 19:25–27 NAB *(italics mine)*

Amid the growing cacophony of human voices all around him, Job cried out to God. Love and desire for the One he had served for so many years consumed him. A desperate resolve took shape within him and it became *God's* voice that he determined to hear, *His* face that he had to see.

In great torment of soul, Job continued to cry out for many days. Questioning, summoning, even challenging God to show Himself in person, Job's desperation made him brave; his pain made him bold.

> Oh, that I had one to hear my case,
> and that my accuser would write out his indictment!
> Even should he contend against me with his great power,
> yet, would that he himself might heed me!
> This is my final plea;
> let the Almighty answer me!
>
> —Job 31:35, 23:6, 31:37 NAB

God responded. In one of the Bible's most profound passages, God comes to Job in the midst of a storm and speaks to him personally. God answers the cry of His servant with a cry of His own:

> Where were you when I founded the earth?
> Tell me, if you have understanding.
> Who determined its size; do you know?
> Have you ever in your lifetime commanded the morning
> and shown the dawn its place . . .
> Have you entered into the sources of the sea,
> or walked about in the depths of the abyss?
> Can you raise your voice among the clouds,
> or veil yourself in the waters of the storm?
> Do you hunt the prey for the lioness
> or appease the hunger of her cubs,
> Who puts wisdom in the heart,
> and gives the cock its understanding?

Who provides nourishment for the ravens
when their young ones cry out to God,
and they rove abroad without food?

—Job 38:4, 5, 12, 16, 34, 39, 36, 41 NAB

One hundred and twenty-six verses record the intensity and breadth of God's response to Job. Stanza by stanza, like laser surgery on a spiritual cataract, God's words carried the razor-sharp edge of His invasive light, cutting, piercing, stripping away the layers of Job's blindness and fog.

These words, though harsh, did not kill Job—they freed him. Though severe, they did not destroy his resolve; instead, they increased his faith. Clearly designed for the heart of a servant who needed assurance of his Master's sovereignty, they restored to Job a sense of God's passionate concern for His creation—of which he was part. They were special words, burning words. Ripping through the bondage of blindness, they set him free; with absolute accuracy they hit their mark and opened for him the eyes of his heart.

In response, a dazzled, humbled Job exclaimed,

I know that you can do all things,
and that no purpose of yours can be hindered.
I have dealt with great things that I do not understand;
things too wonderful for me, which I cannot know.
I had heard of you by word of mouth,
but now my eye has seen you.

—Job 42:2–5 NAB *(italics mine)*

The secondhand reports were over. Job had seen God. The depth of his anguish had driven him far beyond the pleasantries of protocol and, reaching for his beloved Master, Job laid hold. God felt the wild, desperate grasp of His faithful servant's hand and rewarded him with new sight. Though singed in the process, Job finally came face-to-face with the living God.

God was not angry with Job. His rebuke was not rejection. He did not rebuff Job with a flick of His finger and disdainfully shake free of a pesky human's pursuit—He honored him.

God cited Job as an example to the three friends that had come to exhort and advise. To them God said, "I am angry with you . . . for you have not spoken rightly concerning me, as has my servant Job. Now, therefore, . . . let my servant Job pray for you; for his prayer I will accept, not to punish you severely. For you have not spoken rightly concerning me, as has my servant Job" (Job 42:7, 8 NAB).

SOME OF US, like Job, have walked with God for many years. We have believed in Him and served Him faithfully, but God has yet to feel from us the untamed, unrestrained reach of our heart in search of His.

In our desire to be pleasing to Him, we have tried hard to behave well. We have concentrated on being very careful and very good. We have been "good witnesses" and "good stewards," "good Samaritans" and "good examples." We have been good at just about everything, except letting

God feel the tough, tenacious pursuit of a hungry heart.

There's a reason for this. Many of us are afraid of overstepping our bounds—of disturbing God with our desire for Him. We are afraid that even if we call, God will not answer, that even if we reach, He will not respond. As pleasing as we have tried to be, we secretly assume that it will be someone else who gets the "real" response of His voice, or the clear view of His face. In fact, because we know ourselves so well, most of us are privately convinced that we will be the one sure exception to God's willingness to interact.

In light of this, it can seem appropriately selfless, even Christlike, to view any personal interaction that comes from God as intended for someone else's more worthy life, or aimed at someone else's more legitimate need.

Not so. Jesus' own need to see His Father was well documented and real and He admitted it freely—"the Son can do nothing of Himself, unless it is something He sees the Father doing" (John 5:19). He would emerge from long, midnight talks with His Father, and declare, "Whatever the Father does, these things the Son also does" . . . "I and the Father are one" (John 5:19; 10:30). Jesus was never ashamed of His dependence nor shy about openly expressing it.

There is nothing remotely selfless or Christlike about not needing to see God. There is nothing admirable about assuming that someone else is more deserving of that to which we have *all* been given equal access.

Jesus calls us by His own example to be passionate and jealous for our birthright. We were born to see God and to respond to Him. God has called us and saved us; now we must believe that He is also willing for us to see Him as He really is.

I remember a time in my own life when, after a long period of struggle, I knew what it felt like to reach for God with all my heart. It was a hard time for me. When it was over, there wasn't much left of my demure, civilized self. I had become so hungry for a glimpse of Him, so ravaged by my need, that what was appropriate behavior didn't seem to matter anymore.

I had, for a period of months, been struggling to understand what I was reading in the Scriptures. Each time I opened my Bible, I felt like I was reliving a scene from a Dickens novel. In my mind's eye I would see myself standing outside on a cold, snowy night, looking through a window into a warm, firelit room filled with feasting people. They were all sitting at a long wooden table, eating from bright, colorful plates and drinking from fat, full mugs.

Around the table the conversation was rich and lively with laughter, as Someone that I could not see told stories and passed plates heaped with steaming food. Everything inside the room seemed light and warm. Everything outside felt dark, cold, and utterly removed from life.

Over and over throughout that period in my life, as I opened my Bible to read, I saw this scene and felt anew all the same hunger and loneliness it represented. I would read but not understand what I had read. I would study because I knew there was substance to be had, but would always leave empty-handed. Everything I craved was locked behind glass in a room that I could not reach.

This went on for a very long time. Long enough, at least, for me to adjust to the hunger and cold and to make a certain, uneasy peace with being outside instead of in. I became a "watcher," an observer of all that others automatically considered their portion. While they were partaking, I was being "patient"; while they were wrapped in the warmth of fellowship, I had cloaked myself with the cold. Finally, the day came when my bit of peace was shattered and the whole experience became too much for me.

The scene as I saw it that day remained unchanged, except that it seemed there was extra food being served—too much food for the number of people present. Plates were piled high and the overflow that no one had space for was in danger of falling to the floor.

It was then that my heart broke and I began to cry. A deep, savage agony rose up within me and I cried out: "What about *me,* Lord? Don't You see my hunger and my pain? Don't You see that those scraps alone would be enough for me? They would be more than enough for me! Why are You letting them be wasted? I *need* them. Please God, please let me in!"

The page of Isaiah that I cried on was messy with ripples and streaks before it was all over. I remember sitting for a very long time staring at one verse in particular, as if it were a locked door, repeating, "Whatever it takes, let me understand Your Word! Let me sit where You are and hear Your voice; let me see Your face with my own eyes! Please, God!"

When I finally got up from the jumble of paper and tears, a free, airy sort of emptiness blew through my heart, for I had dumped its contents right at the feet of Jesus. It was all out, and I knew He had heard me. My mind, frustrated by months of wrestling with hidden truths, had finally made way for my heart to speak. And, in response, Jesus released to the reach of my heart what He had been reluctant to give to the mere grasp of my mind. My patience had dissipated and in its place was a driving resolve that propelled me forward.

After that, I never again saw pictures of myself when I read the Bible. Instead I heard things. I heard the clanking of dishes all around me; I saw plates being passed and heard stories being told. I still didn't fully understand Isaiah, but I wasn't standing outside in the snow, either. I was sitting inside at a long table by the fire and Someone, who I could now see quite clearly, was passing me plates full of food.

Lest this seem like a too-quick, too-magical account of intimacy with God, please know that I have told only the end of what was a major battle in my life. There were no quick solutions for me. Jesus let me struggle long past what I considered a healthy cutoff, but that's what it took for my heart to break free of its natural restraint and reach toward Him.

Looking back to that time, I can testify that there was nothing arbitrary in God's dealings with me. I believe He intentionally put those pictures in my mind to show me myself. Growing up in the church as I did, many things concerning the Scriptures came my way too easily. Much of what I lived on came through other people after they had done the hard work of studying the Bible for themselves. God had to force me to grow up—and He chose hunger to do it.

Whenever necessary, God wields hunger as a weapon, and He does it purposely. He created us with an appetite for Himself, knowing that He alone can satisfy us. Yes, He intends to use us in each other's lives, but ultimately, it is His hand that feeds us. He insists on presiding over His own table and presenting us with the truth of who He is face-to-face. Now, as always when feeding His disciples, *Jesus* breaks the Bread, *He* serves the Cup, and it is in His presence that we eat and drink our fill.

If it is, then, our desire to see God, if we are longing to hear His voice and see His face, He will help us. He will work with us and do whatever is necessary to cut away the layer of fog that obscures our sight. Through the wisdom of His Word, God will free us to see Him ever more clearly and, having seen, to respond more fully. If we ask, He will do it. If we are honest about our need, He will act.

IN THE NEXT chapter we will see that the "reach of the hungering heart" is not all there is for the Christian. There is more. God has given us the ability to reach to Him in a ministerial fashion that has a powerful impact upon His heart.

12

The Reach of the Ministering Heart

Hunger for God and personal desperation play a vital role in driving us deeper into relationship with Him. Even so, our hearts were designed to do more than simply quest after God. They were designed to ultimately find Him, enter into fellowship, and, from that place of fellowship, minister to Him.

IN THE two preceding chapters we explored what I call the "first reach" of the human heart toward God. The hallmark of reaching for God in this way is a profound sense of personal need and a willingness to express that need honestly and openly.

There is also a "second reach" of the heart. This is an equally aggressive action that is born of gratitude and love, not just of hunger and need. It is a response that ministers to God in a special way because it is not motivated by the desire to escape from pain but by the desire to have an impact upon His heart. It is a reach for God Himself, not just for the relief He can give.

Our hunger, blindness, and desperation are essential in bringing us closer to God, but they can never cause us to love Him. Like fear, they can motivate but never inspire. They can dispel complacency and drive us forward but never force us to trust.

An old, word-of-mouth story about Abraham Lincoln tells of a time when he visited a slave auction. Observing the proceedings from the rear of the crowd, his attention was caught by a strong, defiant young slave girl with sharp, angry eyes. Something in her manner pierced him; the sheer intensity of her gaze spoke to him of the anguish of her captivity and her longing for freedom.

When it was her turn to step to the auction block, he and several others bid. With each rise in price, her hostility grew. Finally Lincoln won, paid the money, and had her brought to him.

She came, rigid with resistance, arms tied behind her back, leg chains dragging.

"Untie her," Lincoln said.

"Oh no, sir!" her auctioneer responded, pulling her forward with a jerk. "She be a wild one! Ain't no end o' trouble in her. Ya best git her home afore ya be takin' her chains off." With that, he secured her to the horse rail, turned, and left.

Lincoln stood quietly for a moment, looking at the young woman. "What is your name?" he asked.

She did not respond.

"What are you called?" he repeated.

Steeling herself for the inevitable blow, she set her jaw, stared at the ground, and said nothing.

Taking the bill of sale from his pocket, Lincoln read it carefully, then marked the bottom with his signature. Slowly he stooped, undid the clasp of her ankle irons, and untied the rope that had cut into her wrists.

"You're free to go, Sara-Jane," he said, handing her the document. "You are free to choose your own life now."

Reaching again into his pocket, he drew out a card and several coins. "If you have any trouble," he said, "call on me at this address and I will help you."

As the reality of what she had heard seeped slowly through her brain and into her muscles, the young woman grew weak and unable to sustain her rage. Minutes ticked by as anger gave way to confusion and confusion to disbelief. Like someone in the grip of a personal earthquake, her face spasmed, then settled again; her muscular shoulders convulsed, then were still. Finally, a large, work-calloused hand rose to take the papers and the money. Instantly, she turned and ran.

Lincoln watched as she disappeared down the mud-rutted road. Taking the reigns of his horse, he began to mount when he saw her suddenly stop.

Some distance away, she stood totally still. More minutes passed. Then, slowly, deliberately, she made her way back. Standing in front of him, she handed him the money.

"I choose you," she said, looking up for the first time into Lincoln's gaunt, craggy face. "You say I choose my own life now," she continued haltingly, ". . . that I work for who I want. You give me papers to show that I be free." The deep sinkholes of her oval face were wet with emotion. "If that be true . . . if I be free . . . then I choose you!"

Whether fact or fiction, this story illustrates someone's free choice toward relationship even after their need had been met. It is, I believe, a good example for those of us who follow Jesus because, in the same way, it is ultimately our pursuit of relationship, not just rescue, that ministers to God.

WHEN WE minister to God with the second reach of our heart, we willingly enter the realm of relationship. We acknowledge something between us that is deeper and more binding than a simple acceptance of assistance; we do more than think nice thoughts about the person who has helped us—we choose to rise and reach again.

After healing the ten lepers who had come to Him for help, Jesus experienced the "second reach" from only one of the ten. All ten men rejoiced in their newly found health, all were excited and grateful, but only one returned to Jesus and thanked Him personally. Only one pursued the source of his healing and intentionally reached again.

This is the nature of the second reach, that our focus shifts, our gaze gains altitude, and we return not only to receive from the hand of God but to touch the heart of God. In so doing, we acknowledge that we can have an impact upon God, not just He on us. We recognize a bond between us that is more exacting than that of services-rendered/thank-you-notes-sent. We acknowledge that, by virtue of His entering our world to become like us, Jesus now has the right to draw us into His world to become like Him.

Let me illustrate this point. It is, I believe, the first reach of the heart toward God that we have seen so graphically and movingly demonstrated year after year in Billy Graham crusades. Huge stadiums packed with people streaming down the aisles singing "Just as I Am" reflect an enormous, widespread hunger for God and desire for His help. All over the world, thousands of people congregate at the front of auditoriums and open-air stadiums because they are desperate and needy, wanting forgiveness and healing.

It is, however, the second reach of the heart that comes due when the immediate crisis has passed, everyone has returned home, and daily life begins again. And, I believe it is because of this that Billy Graham faithfully refers not only to "the moment of salvation" but to "the hour of decision." Evangelist though he is, he knows that the second reach of the heart toward God, the choice to pursue an ongoing, faith-filled relationship, stretches far beyond the emotion-filled moment of an altar call.

In the story of the prodigal son, we get another glimpse of this truth. As the younger, rebellious son of a wealthy merchant returned home starving, exhausted, and penniless, having spent much of his father's fortune, he was met on the road and welcomed even before he could speak all his words of repentance. So full was his father's forgiveness that, as the young man was still begging for mercy and a place of servanthood, he was joyfully received back as a son.

His father's own robe was flung around his shoulders, his father's ring was placed on his finger, and new sandals were placed on his feet. Servants were then sent scurrying to prepare a grand feast of celebration.

If the story had continued to follow this young man, however, I imagine we would have seen another dynamic take place in his heart. I believe he would have eventually been escorted past the moment of his salvation and brought to the hour of decision. He would have faced the challenge to rise and reach again.

This time he, like his older brother before him, would be called upon to share in the full responsibility of relationship with his father. He would be asked to reach, not out of personal need but in acceptance of sonship, not because it quelled the inner urgency of his own desperation, but because, with his father's robe on his back, ring on his finger, and blessing on his head, he was a living expression of his father's forgiving heart. He was a recipient of, and therefore a responder to, his father's all-embracing nature.

In rising and reaching again, he would become the beneficiary of something more loving, more binding, more extravagantly inclusive than a mere rescue operation. No longer would he be allowed to see himself as a tail-between-the-legs prodigal but as a fully responsible partner in his father's household. However unworthy he felt, he would be caretaker and *partaker* of his father's wealth—a trusted participant with him in managing all that he held dear. Such is the exacting nature of the grace by which we stand. We are called as sons, not just servants; we are called to celebrate, not just survive.

I HAVE EXPERIENCED "the hour of decision" in my own life. It has, in fact, stretched over the many years of my walk with the Lord. I know what it is to feel both the first and second "reaches" of the heart.

As explained in earlier chapters, I have felt the kind of driving need that cries out for rescue and relief. And, I have known the equally relentless pull of the Holy Spirit urging me to pursue more than just relief.

Though I have never made my way down the aisle of a Billy Graham crusade, I have, in times of personal crisis, sung the words of that same, wonderful old hymn as I walked the aisles of my own heart . . .

"Just as I am, without one plea,
But that thy blood was shed for me,
And that thou bid'st me come to thee,
O Lamb of God, I come, I come."

—Charlotte Elliot, 1789-1871

When I have come to God with these words, I have sensed His acceptance of me. Just like scruffy little Zaccheus and desperate old Job, my own scruffy, desperate heart has been heard and answered. Just like the tired young prodigal, God has responded to my reach toward Him and I have been accepted and loved.

I have, however, at the very moment of God's acceptance, also been challenged to rise and reach again. Even as I hear the Lord saying, "Yes, child, come to Me just as you are—broken, needy, and riddled with weakness and fear," I hear these next words ". . . and then let Me come to you just as *I Am*, complete in My strength and sufficiency, majestic in My power and provision. Yes, come in your weakness but then make room for Me to come in My strength; you come to Me with your sin and grief but then make way for Me to come to you with the fire of My forgiveness and joy!"

By simply expressing the desire to be accepted by God unconditionally—just as I really am—the challenge comes for me to accept *Him* unconditionally—just as *He* really is.

Suddenly it is not enough that I receive comfort. Instead, I am being asked to reach up and receive Him, the God of all comfort. It is not enough that I find answers to my questions, healing for my hurts, and forgiveness for my sins. I have been called into relationship with Jesus and it is clear that, as I rise and reach again, it will be to receive the fullness of all that He is—not just the benefits of all that He does. Like the prodigal, the decision involves sonship, not just servanthood.

THE SECOND reach has always been difficult for me. I have found it difficult to make way for the Lord to come to me just as He is. It has, in fact, taken more faith for me to receive God in all of His glory than it has for me to trust that He will receive me with all of my failure and sin. After all (I say to myself) He is God and all things are possible with Him. But I am only frail humanity. How can I hope to contend with the full force of His divine nature? How can even my huge hollowness of soul be space enough to harbor His manifest glory?

Instinctively I know that if I make way for Jesus to come to me "just as He is," I will no longer be just as I am—I will be changed. I will no longer be in control of me—God will be.

This is a crucial point of reckoning—this is my hour of decision. Will I reach once or twice? Will I pursue Jesus just long enough to feel better or will I stay and be changed? Am I going to opt for the cozy campfire of His presence or for the full, towering fire of His passionate nature?

The very act of staying in His presence, of reaching to Him again, ministers to God, because it invites His full influence in my life. It says that I want to be like Jesus and am ready to embrace the whole of who He is. It says that I want relationship, not just rescue.

I HAVE MADE this choice on several occasions during my life but, as I say, it has been hard for me. I have needed help. In the next chapter we will see how faithful God is in extending His hand to help us move toward relationship with Him. We will see that it is ultimately *He* who bridges the gap between the first and second reaches of our heart.

13

FREEDOM TEACHER

There is a time of transition in the life of a Christian whenever God leads from the first reach of the heart to the second. Though this transition can be gentle and largely uneventful, for many of us it is a difficult, unsettling time.

It is a time when God challenges every former security and draws us, one bewildering birth contraction after another, into the world outside the womb of self-absorption.

YOU MUST let me have her completely to myself, Captain Keller; Helen must learn to depend upon me for everything. If she needs food she must come to me. If she needs water she must receive it from me. For training, help, love, sleep—for everything—it must be to me that she turns."

Anne Sullivan stood facing her employer squarely, her young head erect, her Irish jaw set.

For a week since her arrival at the Keller home in Tuscumbia, Alabama, she had tried without success to penetrate her seven-year-old student's angry inner world. Five years earlier, in February of 1882, Helen Keller had been stricken with a near-fatal illness. When her fever finally broke and the illness lifted, Helen, who had been a normal, active toddler, was completely blind and deaf.

Overnight her tiny body became a sealed time capsule for one of the most eager intellects of her generation. It would require a special teacher with a special kind of love to unlock all that was now lying trapped within its sightless, soundless walls.

Outwardly, Helen became a tyrant. Her family considered her so pitiful and in need of protection that no one was allowed to discipline her. In the name of love, her every whim was indulged and every foul mood forgiven. Left unchecked, her tantrums escalated until no one in the household dared deny her anything. Instead, she was allowed to roam free of all restraint, groping from room to room, banging on walls when angry, toppling furniture when bored, and freely foraging for food when hungry. The older she grew the more wild and dangerous her outbursts became.

One day, incensed that her newborn sister was sleeping peacefully in a cradle she often used for her doll, Helen rushed at the tiny bed in a rage and overturned it. Mrs. Keller caught baby Mildred just in time to save her life.

On another occasion, Helen discovered how to use a key, then locked her mother in the pantry. For three hours Mrs. Keller pounded on the door while Helen sat on the steps outside, laughing gleefully and enjoying the feel of the vibrations coming through the porch floor.

Eventually, the Kellers became convinced that a tutor was needed to help civilize their daughter. With the assistance of Dr. Alexander Graham Bell, they located Anne Sullivan and brought her to Alabama from Boston's Perkins Institution for the Blind.

SHORTLY AFTER her new teacher arrived, Helen followed her to her room, slammed the door, locked it from the outside, and hid the key under the wardrobe in the hall. No amount of coaxing could induce Helen to reveal where she had hidden the key, so Captain Keller was compelled to get a ladder and carry Miss Sullivan out through the upstairs window. Helen was delighted. Months later she produced the key.

This prank set the tone for the new student/teacher relationship, and the two spent their first few days engaged in combat. The following excerpt was taken from one of Miss Sullivan's letters written just after her arrival at the Keller homestead:

"I had a battle royal with Helen this morning. Although I try very hard not to force issues, I find it very difficult to avoid them.

"Helen's table manners are appalling. She puts her hands in our plates and helps herself, and when

the dishes are passed, she grabs them and takes out whatever she wants. This morning I would not let her put her hand in my plate. She persisted, and a contest of wills followed. Naturally the family was much disturbed, and left the room.

"I locked the dining-room door, and proceeded to eat my breakfast, though the food almost choked me. Helen was lying on the floor, kicking and screaming and trying to pull my chair from under me. She kept this up for half an hour, then she got up to see what I was doing. I let her see that I was eating, but did not let her put her hand in the plate. She pinched me, and I slapped her every time she did it.

"Then she went all round the table to see who was there, and finding no one but me, she seemed bewildered. After a few minutes she came back to her place and began to eat her breakfast with her fingers. I gave her a spoon, which she threw on the floor. I forced her out of the chair and made her pick it up. Finally I succeeded in getting her back in her chair again, and held the spoon in her hand, compelling her to take up the food with it and put it in her mouth. In a few minutes she yielded and finished her breakfast peaceably.

"Then we had another tussle over folding her napkin. When she had finished, she threw it on the floor and ran toward the door. Finding it locked, she began to kick and scream all over again. It was another hour before I succeeded in getting her napkin folded.

"Then I let her out into the warm sunshine and went up to my room and threw myself on the bed

exhausted. I had a good cry and felt better. I suppose I shall have many such battles with the little woman before she learns the only two essential things I can teach her, obedience and love." [1]

THE TEACHING of these two essentials was slow going with Helen. Obedience was actively avoided and every overture of affection rejected. Accompanying Helen's own reluctance to be taught was constant, though well intentioned, interference from family members. Neither Captain nor Mrs. Keller could stand to see their daughter disciplined. Each time Helen lost a battle, she would run to her parents for sympathy and consolation.

Now, some days after her arrival, Miss Sullivan was still working hard to make her authority felt. It was at this point that she approached the Kellers for time alone with Helen in a nearby cottage. They agreed.

As difficult as it was for them, they made preparations for Helen to be handed over to the sole care of her teacher. It was agreed that during a two-week period of time they would not interfere in any way. They could visit and watch Helen from a distance but not let her know of their presence. Meals were to be brought to the cottage by the household servants, but even they were not allowed to touch Helen or let her know they were nearby. Only Miss Sullivan was allowed near her.

After her arrival at the cottage, Helen was outraged to find herself confined to a small, cramped

[1] Keller, Helen, *The Story of My Life* (Garden City: Doubleday, 1954), p. 248.

space with only her bullheaded teacher. Her tantrums increased. Removed from everything most familiar, she became homesick, disoriented, and sullen. She was angered by any attempt at interaction.

This did not deter her teacher. In every corner of the cottage, Miss Sullivan's persistent hand came seeking Helen's tiny, rebellious fist. Relentlessly it came, repeating over and over in sign language the names of objects in the cottage. Everywhere Helen went, she was required to listen to the silent, manual language of the deaf.

Every time Helen had a need and imperiously demanded that it be met, she was given the name of what she was demanding before her desire was fulfilled. If it was food that she wanted, she was force-fed the name of what she was eating, along with the food itself. If it was a toy she desired, first the name, then the toy itself, was given to her. Nothing was available to her just for the taking. If she had a need, she had to interact.

Helen grew increasingly frustrated at each new onslaught of communication. She shunned "the hand" that was always moving in mysterious, incomprehensible formations. Repeatedly she pulled away and sank more deeply and dejectedly into herself.

As her homesickness grew, the battle raged around the clock. Day and night ran together as teacher and student fought with increasing ferocity and primal wit. Finally, thoroughly exhausted, Helen's resistance crumbled and she succumbed to a hard-won understanding—Miss Sullivan was in charge; she was not.

With this foundation finally in place, things went more smoothly. Helen became more compliant. Though she had no understanding of what she was doing, she learned to sign several words back into her teacher's hand. As yet, no connection existed for her between the doll in her arms and the word "d-o-l-l" that she could make with her fingers. The fact that everything had a name was still unknown to her.

Nevertheless, by the end of the two weeks Helen had changed remarkably. Anne Sullivan's letter of March 20, 1887, records her progress:

"My heart is singing for joy this morning. A miracle has happened! The light of understanding has shone upon my little pupil's mind, and behold, all things are changed!

"The wild little creature of two weeks ago has been transformed into a gentle child. She is sitting by me as I write, her face serene and happy, crocheting a long red chain of Scotch wool. . . .

"She lets me kiss her now, and when she is in a particularly gentle mood, she will sit in my lap for a minute or two; but she does not return my caresses. The great step—the step that counts—has been taken. The little savage has learned her first lesson in obedience, and finds the yoke easy." [2]

THE KELLERS were thrilled with their new, civilized little girl. Though much was left to be accomplished in the cottage and Miss Sullivan

[2] Ibid, p. 252.

begged for more time, the family insisted that Helen be allowed to come home.

The entire household celebrated her return with great rejoicing. In the cottage, Helen had learned many of the social refinements of a normal child her age. She sat at her place during meals, ate with silverware, and folded her napkin when she finished. She washed and dressed herself, combed her own hair, and picked up her toys. The experiment was a great success. Victory was clear—Helen had been tamed.

Miss Sullivan, however, was far from satisfied. This was not the end, but the beginning of her work. Obedience and the compliance it produced were not her final goals but the keys necessary to unlock prison doors. The bondage of Helen's raging rebellion had been broken but the capsule containing her heart and mind was still tightly sealed. Behind the vacant stare still lived a lonely, frightened little girl waiting to be found and freed.

Like a small landing between flights of stairs, Helen's polite, civilized behavior was only a place to rest and change direction before climbing higher. It was intended as part of a process—not her final destination.

So, day after day, teacher and student doggedly continued to pantomime the process of communication. Hour after hour their hands continued to move through seemingly meaningless gestures, waiting for the moment of flashing inner connection to come. It came on April 5, 1887:

"I must write you a line this morning because something very important has happened. Helen has taken the second great step in her education. She has learned that everything has a name, and that the manual alphabet is the key to everything she wants to know. . . .

"We went out to the pump-house, and I made Helen hold her mug under the spout while I pumped. As the cold water gushed forth, filling the mug, I spelled 'w-a-t-e-r' in Helen's free hand. The word coming so close upon the sensation of cold water rushing over her hand seemed to startle her. She dropped the mug and stood as one transfixed. A new light came into her face. She spelled 'water' several times. Then she dropped on the ground and asked for its name and pointed to the pump and the trellis, and suddenly turning round she asked for my name. I spelled 'Teacher'. . .

"P.S.—I didn't finish my letter in time to get it posted last night; so I shall add a line. Helen got up this morning like a radiant fairy. She has flitted from object to object, asking the name of everything and kissing me for very gladness. Last night when I got in bed, she stole into my arms of her own accord and kissed me for the first time, and I thought my heart would burst, so full was it of joy." [3]

THIS EVENT marked the beginning of one of the world's most famous friendships—and the lifetime of wondrous freedom it produced. Through the gift of communication, Miss Sullivan led Helen out

[3] Ibid, p. 256.

of her tight, confining darkness into the spacious world beyond.

She taught Helen to write English and to read braille, then sent her on forays into the land of letters and books. Using words, Anne Sullivan carved for Helen's thoughts a passageway into the light, then watched as the light of other's thoughts reached her student in return. She taught Helen sign language, lipreading, and how to speak, then ushered her into the richly patterned parlor of human conversation.

At the age of twenty-two, while still a sophomore in college, Helen astounded the entire educational community by publishing her first book. Two years later, in 1904, she did what no one thought possible; she graduated from Radcliffe—with honors.

After college this same girl, who as a child had groped blindly from room to room throughout her parents' home, traveled extensively throughout the world. With her teacher by her side, she visited over twenty-five countries, met with heads of state, and was decorated with numerous medals of distinction.

Ironically, Helen Keller, the wild little "savage" who had once taken such joy in locking her teacher in a room, had been *un*locked by her in return. Through a love equal to her own stubbornness, she was released from the bondage of her body to become one of this century's most accomplished communicators. Over the course of her lifetime, Miss Keller received global acclaim as a lecturer, author, and tireless humanitarian. Her twelve books and numerous articles have been translated into more than fifty languages, and the effect of her loving service on behalf of the handicapped is still felt by millions worldwide.

All this was waiting on the other side of a cottage door. Though Helen could not have known it then, on the other side of disorientation and pain were freedom and new life. Great liberty followed the hated rigors of confinement, and the same hand that held the keys to freedom first tormented with bitter, unrelenting confrontation.

In the cottage, the driving force of Helen's physical needs compelled her to break through to the first reach of the heart. Then, in the equally bewildering weeks that followed, her teacher built a bridge for the second reach of her heart that was yet to come. The cottage was not a place of punishment but of preparation; the weeks following were not spent polishing hard-won social skills but pursuing the language of life itself.

To any with a less-demanding love, the accomplishment of a quiet, correct life filled with proper behavior would have been enough. For many who knew Helen best, a tame, gentler child could easily have seemed like the pinnacle of success.

Helen's teacher was different. She wanted more. Helen's teacher wanted her *free*!

WE HAVE a Teacher who wants His people free. Jesus wants more for us than tame, civilized behavior and the "shoulds" of the Christian life. He wants true communication, genuine heart responses—not just polished, monkey-like imitations of a reality we don't yet share.

For most of us, the path to freedom leads through the cottage. In order to accomplish our ultimate release, Jesus often removes us from that which is most secure and emotionally familiar. He takes us from the soft, indulgent arms that have become our home and sequesters us with Himself.

Locked in a strange, foreign place where everything is threatening and new, our Teacher waits for the real "us" to emerge. There in the face of our raw, screaming need and dark, rebellious anger, He begins to meet with us, unhindered by the kind of "love" for which comfort is more valued than communion.

When we are hungry, it is His hand that feeds us; when we are thirsty, it is He who gives us something cool to drink; when we are tired from our tantrums, it is Jesus Himself who makes a place for us to rest. Everywhere we turn He is there, His hand in our hand, maddeningly, unrelentingly spelling new, mysterious words of life.

Most of us don't respond well to this place of disorientation and forced communication. We are angry and in pain. We don't recognize where we are or even why we're there. We just know that something has gone terribly wrong with our safe, familiar world. Perhaps our relationships are crumbling, our finances failing, or our health deteriorating. Maybe after twenty years at the same job our competence is being questioned and our worth reassessed. Those systems that were once our strongest means of identity and support are now just a point of painful, wistful recollection. Like Helen, we are frightened and homesick. We want to go back to being loved in the old familiar ways that allowed us to remain emotionally unchallenged and internally unchanged.

Once in the cottage, however, we almost never come out unchanged. For most of us it is a profoundly transforming experience. If we enter as an unbeliever, it is not unusual to "meet" the Lord in that place and experience His saving grace. If we enter as a nominal, inactive Christian, we often emerge energized, more committed and active in the things of the church. If we go in as an already active, committed follower of Jesus Christ, we come out stripped of all our formulas for living the Christian life and newly dependent upon Jesus for everything.

Whatever individual changes the cottage may produce in us, when we finally emerge, we are faced with yet another surprise. Like little Helen, we're amazed to find that for all the trauma we've just endured, our Teacher's work has only begun. In spite of our recent breakthrough (whatever it may be) the bewildering hand signals don't stop. Even though we're using all of our newly acquired table manners and social skills, the lesson isn't over.

Because we don't understand the true nature of our Teacher's love, we underestimate the full scope of His plan. We often pass through our prison-like struggle still unclear about the goals of the One with whom we've been confined. We think all He cares about is that we "get saved" or become a more productive, obedient disciple. We mistakenly assume that all the battles and mysterious hand signals have been for the primary purpose of making us more compliant at the dinner table, more presentable in public.

Unaware of the rest of our Teacher's agenda, we begin to rely on simple, behavioral changes. We go to church, smile a lot, and say nice things. We read our Bible and witness more. We work hard at being helpful. We stay in our seat, eat with a spoon, and fold our napkin when we're finished.

This makes many people happy. We're so much improved over the "old" us that the grand experiment is declared a success. Jesus "works"; we've been changed.

The only problem with all this personal improvement is that we have a Teacher who wants more—we have a Teacher who wants us free!

Jesus' plan is much bigger than most of us initially understand. When He closes the cottage door and starts talking to us, it is not for strict behavioral and attitudinal change—it is for freedom. The words that Jesus spoke two thousand years ago are still true today, "If therefore the Son shall make you free, you shall be free indeed" (John 8:36).

Even after the moment of our salvation, even after the decision to embrace genuine commitment and active church involvement, even after we come to a point of total trust in Him—Jesus wants more. He wants us free to speak the language of the heart.

Jesus is not satisfied that we're easier to control and nicer to be around; He wants us free to converse and commune. He's not interested in holding us hostage by the sheer force of our own need; He wants us healed and whole. Jesus isn't even content that we've found in Him a place of security and shelter from the storms of life; He wants us free to venture back out into life's risky, loveless waters—taking His love with us as we go.

Jesus wants more for the adulterer than the relinquishing of a mistress—He wants him healed enough to embrace the intimacy of marriage. He wants more for the alcoholic than iron-willed sobriety—He wants him free to face life without emotional escape. He wants more for the troubled Christian than a white-knuckled wait until heaven—He wants him free to pursue all that the Father has put here on earth. In short, the person that the Teacher tangles with in the confines of the cottage will not just be free of painful compulsions and a fear-filled future, he or she will be free to commune with the living God!

Jesus purposely takes us to the cottage and battles with us there because, at the very point of our greatest wounding, He wants to give us words. He wants to give language to the locked places of our heart—to talk to us and to hear us talk back. His goal is to find and free the lonely, lost parts of us that were sealed by sickness long ago—to penetrate our inner darkness with light, our soul-silence with sound.

Whatever the cottage may be like for us, this is its fundamental purpose. It is for freedom that we have been brought to this place of confinement and confrontation. Yes, our time there is often brutal and bewildering. It is, however, not a place to fear, for whenever we are with our Teacher we are under love's jurisdiction—and true love allows no haphazard destruction.

By whatever circumstances Satan may have intended our harm, God accomplishes His own plan of healing and health. Wherever evil seeks to destroy, God moves to restore; and it is in the very presence of death that God brings us to newness of life (Gen. 45:4–8).

God never wastes our pain. In His skillful, loving hand the enemy's dagger becomes a surgeon's scalpel. His searing heat wounds only in order to heal. He crushes, only to create anew all that was originally intended to be. His love defends while it disciplines, protects while it purifies, and invades the safety of the shell, only that the pearl may go free.

IF YOU HAVE ever been to the cottage, you know that it is often in this place of pain and great struggle that Jesus begins to build the bridge that connects the first reach of the heart to the second. This is the scope of His plan. Ultimately, Jesus wants us free enough to rise and reach again of our own accord. He wants us able to say with Israel of old,

> "Come, let us return to the Lord.
> For He has torn us, but He will heal us;
> He has wounded us, but He will bandage us.
> He will revive us after two days;
> He will raise us up on the third day
> That we may live before Him.
> So let us know, let us press on to know the Lord.
> His going forth is as certain as the dawn;
> And He will come to us like the rain,
> Like the spring rain watering the earth."
>
> —Hosea 6:1–3

Like newly-transformed little Helen Keller crawling into her teacher's arms at last, Jesus wants to feel the second reach of our heart coming to Him in full embrace. He wants to hear each of us say, "I will return to the Lord—yes, I will know, I will press on to *know* the Lord!"

Coming to Jesus in this way, with eager arms outstretched, tells Him that we are ready. Ready not only to be loved but to love; ready not only for rescue but for relationship. The second reach of the heart tells Jesus we are ready to explore with Him the vast world of His Father's kingdom, to follow Him to that place of fire and fellowship where everything has a name, where every symbol has substance and every movement has meaning.

There He will walk with us and talk with us. There, as the Scriptures say, He will abide in us (John 15:4). With His hand in ours, Jesus will continue loving us, teaching us, *freeing* us—to learn the ancient languages of His heart.

14

BECAUSE YOU LOVE THE MUSIC

"As I wander through the dark, encountering difficulties . . . I sense a holy passion pouring down from the springs of Infinity. I thrill to music that beats with the pulses of God. Bound to suns and planets by invisible cords, I feel the flame of eternity in my soul." [1] *—Helen Keller*

AS OUR TEACHER builds the bridge between the first reach of our heart and the second, we begin to hear The Music coming to us from the other side. Those truths that speak of God's purposes and His pleasure become ever more accessible and

[1] *The Open Door* (Garden City: Doubleday, 1957), p. 136.

understandable to us. Our vision clears and we begin to see things from more than just an earthly perspective. Though perhaps still trapped in physical circumstances beyond our control, our spirit is able to travel freely with the Holy Spirit into the furnace of fellowship.

This is God's doing. It is His provision for us. We cannot build our own bridge—only He can; we cannot find our own way—only He can lead us.

Even when we are in so much pain that all we care about is rescue, if we call out to Him, He will lead us to relationship. If, in a time of crisis, we stretch to Him with the first reach of our heart, He will lead us to the second. He is always faithful to do so. The Bible tells us that God is faithful to bring to completion all that He has begun in us (Phil. 1:6).

Once the bridge is built, however, it is we who must choose to cross it. Once we recognize that it is God Himself who is talking to us, it is we who must choose to rise and reach again. This is our part and no one can do it for us. Ultimately it is up to each of us to view our purpose as more important than our pain. The call of God on our lives to stand before Him as ministers to Him must be acknowledged and answered by each of us individually, regardless of our circumstances.

As we answer God's call to ministry, we are not assigned some daunting, difficult task. In order to cross the bridge from the first reach of the heart to the second, we do not need to struggle and strain to "do" something magnificent and spiritual—instead we simply agree with God about who we are to Him. We come like a little child ready to hear His heart and agree with His Word. We come ready to share in His compassions, participate in His purposes, and reflect back to Him the passions of His heart. We choose to leave behind old notions of inadequacy and embrace the priestly person that God called us to be.

IN ALL OF THIS, God's Spirit is our constant helper and guide. He helps us by birthing in us a great love for what God loves. He creates in us an acute longing to hear more of The Music—the Godhead's own celebration song. And He guides us by stirring to life the desire to be part of all that we hear.

Most of us hear faint strains of The Music very early in our Christian walk. Wafting in and around the buzz of everyday life like the aroma of bread from a baker's oven, it captures our senses and awakens a deep longing. Often, during times of worship when our inner noise falls silent, we hear again the familiar, far-off refrain and turn, like a child toward home, at the sound of Someone calling our name.

Over weeks, months, and sometimes years, the Holy Spirit fans into flame our desire to hear more of this music that we were created to sing. It is not, however, until we come to the cottage that many of us begin to hear The Music with clarity and consistency. Though hardly in the mood to answer its summons to celebration at that time, we still sense in our Teacher's unrelenting pursuit its familiar, recurring theme. And, as we respond to our Teacher's touch, we find The Music coming closer—lasting longer.

As the bridge of communication is built, and as we rise to reach again, we begin to hear the ocean-like cadence of this ancient song surging in our own inner ear. The jubilant, unbreakable bond of love between the Father, Son, and Holy Spirit begins to swirl around us with great strength. It captures us and draws us in.

Suddenly we're not just hearing The Music—we're part of The Music! We're not just reaching for what satisfies our heart, we're entering the celebration of God's heart! From earth we're drawn into the activity of heaven, and a potent, participatory love replaces the lonely longing that we once knew. As this love for God and His music grows, much of what we do as ministry to Him follows quite naturally.

IN CHAPTER TWO, I spoke of my cousin Eric and a musical symposium he led at the University near our home. You will recall that Eric was on a brief tour of the Midwestern states and had agreed to lead a master class in trombone while in Iowa City. He played some selected pieces and lectured briefly. Now I would like to finish the story of that afternoon.

After Eric's lecture, several students requested that he listen to them play, then critique what he heard. As I listened to the auditions, one particular young man stands out in my memory. During this student's presentation of the trombone solo from Rimsky-Korsakov's Russian Easter Overture, Eric listened attentively. When he finished, Eric asked him to play the piece again.

"Did you know," he asked as the student finished for the second time, "that each time you played the ninth and tenth measures, you rushed through the rests? The part calls for three full beats of rest and you played only about a beat and a half."

The student reviewed the place on the page where Eric was pointing.

"That oversight could seem trivial," Eric continued, "but it is actually very important. In fact, in this piece it would be disastrous to rush the allotted time of the rest."

Eric looked up at the class.

"You see, during this brief, seemingly unimportant rest, the cello section makes an incredibly beautiful chord change. If the trombone soloist comes in early with the remainder of the solo, the whole effect will have been ruined. No one will hear the cellos; their moment will pass and the overall beauty of the composition will suffer."

Turning back to the student, Eric said, "I want you to find a recording of this piece and listen to it over and over until your heart begins to respond to every note. Play it in the morning when you get up, during the day as you drive to class, and again at night as you fall asleep. Play it until you can feel the music in the deepest part of you and know, without actually hearing it, how it should sound. I want you to learn to love this music—all of it—not just the part that the trombones play."

"If you do this," Eric continued, "if you train your ear to love this entire piece of music, you will be able to play your part with the full accuracy and impact that it requires. *Because* you love the music, you will not rush through the rests. In fact, because you love the music, you will instinctively play in such a way as to protect the other instruments around you. You will play your part just as the composer intended—just as it was written."

WHEN JESUS walked on the earth, He played His part just as it was written. He came as the Messiah, the God-man who would take away the sins of the world. Though He was King, He took the role of servant; though He was sovereign, He submitted to suffering. He, the eternal One, took on finite form and purchased with love the allegiance He had every right to require by force.

Because He loved The Music, He did everything precisely as it was written in the Scriptures. Not once did He deviate. Even as He ended His ministry among men and made His way to the cross, Jesus continued in His ministry to His Father by fulfilling every prophetic detail as foretold in the Scriptures. From the act of riding into Jerusalem on the back of a donkey to standing silently before His accusers, He did everything according to plan. He went, as Isaiah had prophesied centuries before, "like a lamb that is led to slaughter" (Isa. 53:7).

It has always been Jesus' grand passion to do His Father's will and to please His Father's heart. This He did by playing The Music just as it was written. Through the uncompromising obedience of the Son, the glorious music of the Godhead was given full expression all the way to the cross—and beyond.

WE, THE CHURCH, are now the earthly expression of that eternal love song. It is we who now play The Music and, like the young University student, if we are to play with the accuracy and passion it deserves, we must expose our hearts to the constant influence of its beauty and power. By personal, ongoing exposure to all that the Bible says, we will find ourselves responding eagerly to every ageless note, every shift in cadence—every changing chord.

In this way, as we grow in our love for all that is written, several things happen to us simultaneously. First, we begin to play The Music with the same impact that Jesus' earthly life had. We resonate with the same love Jesus had for His Father as well as for the world He died to save. Our lives begin to have an impact on heaven as well as on earth.

As we learn to carry within us a true, deep love for *all* that has been written, our ministry to God will be much more than an exclusive, ivory-tower interaction with Him alone; it will be a loving, vibrant infiltration of the lives of those around us.

By loving what God loves, we will avoid the false, super-spiritual trap of "ministering to God" while selfishly, selectively separating ourselves from that which He holds dear. In fact, because of our love for The Music, broken homes and hearts will be touched by its healing refrain; empty, echoing lives will be given a strong new voice, and the salvation song of Jesus will continue to resound in the earth. Guarded by our love for God—and all that He loves—our ministry to Him will remain open, free-flowing, broadly inclusive, and clearly reflective of His love for the world.

Though our ministry to God does not depend upon human need nor does it have to intersect with human need to be valid, for those who love The Music, ministering to God and ministering to mankind are not mutually exclusive activities. Instead, like the skillfully penned notes of a great symphony, they are intricately interwoven.

Secondly, because we love the Composer and all that He has written, we will rejoice in the part we've been given to play—however great or small. Secure in the ultimate importance of what we've been called to do, we will encourage and applaud the contributions of all those around us.

We will protect every other instrument. Every other person who follows Jesus as Savior and Lord, every other congregation of believers, regardless of denominational affiliation, will be honored in the part they've been given to play. Though we may sound as different from each other as a tuba and a triangle, if we are in the same orchestra, playing with the same, genuine love for The Music, the differences will be woven into one whole, harmonic sound.

This we can trust God to do. We can trust Him to conduct what He has composed and to guide that for which He gave His life. If we watch Him closely, He will lead us. He will tell each of us when to play and when to rest, when to proceed and when to stop and simply listen—as the cellos make their chord change.

Finally, and most importantly, because we love The Music, we will have the courage to follow wherever it may lead. We will have the courage and power to enter the furnace of fellowship and take part in the great exchange-of-hearts.

Because we love God and The Music He has written, we will have the priestly authority to minister directly to Him. We will become those who carry in our hearts the very heart of the God in whom we delight.

EPILOGUE

I would like to say a final word to those readers who may reach the end of this book and say, "OK! OK! I'm ready to minister to God, so give me the specifics—tell me what to *do!*"

As someone who also struggles with a desire for the "how-to's" of Christian living, it is tempting to write a few more chapters and try to answer that question. My walk with God, however, has proven to me that formulas and faith rarely blend and hold for any length of time.

Is there more to be said about ministering to God? Yes. With God there is always more, and in His grace He seems willing for us to talk among ourselves about the practicalities of any truth.

This, on the other hand, is not primarily a "how-to" book. While hoping to give some constructive guidance along the way, my purpose has been to lay a foundation for the concept of ministering to God, understanding in advance that He alone can supply the details of how each of us should build. I look forward to the day when more can be written without being distracting or counterproductive to the individuality of this process.

In the meantime, I can offer this—the God that we serve is jealous for our affection and committed to personal interaction. He is purposeful in His callings, creative in His communication and ever willing to do a new thing in the lives of His people. He is the Great Teacher, and as we reach our hand to His, He will begin to reveal—in ways that are uniquely meaningful to each of us—the part we've been given to play in ministering to Him.